Ready to fast track your success?

This book's your ticket!

- It's the ultimate road map to achieving your goals.

- It offers hundreds of indispensible prospecting tips and strategies.

- It's an indispensible tool for building — and training — your downline.

- It's a great source of inspiration and motivation.

- It's what you need to join network marketing's elite.

Absolutely EVERYTHING You Need to Know About Prospecting

The winning strategies today's top earners use to make friends,
recruit distributors and build their network marketing empires

Russ Johnson, Ph.D. and Usa Johnson
with Beth Mende Conny

Absolutely Everything *You Need to Know About Prospecting*

For permissions, contact:

Biz Builders Consulting, LLC
P.O. Box 1936
Frederick, MD 21702
301/694-9921
BizBuildersConsulting.com

Cover and interior design by SheefishGraphics.com

Neither the authors nor publishers intend this publication to predict the incomes of individuals participating in network marketing or encourage the involvement with a particular network marketing company. Examples included in this book are for illustrative purposes only. No individual should elect to participate in a network marketing opportunity without careful research and consideration.

Dedication

To our families with love and appreciation, and to our family of network marketers worldwide, whose commitment and vision continue to inspire us.

Contents

Acknowledgments

Network marketing is a people business, and it's been our honor to have met so many wonderful people over the years. In large and small ways, they helped us build our business and create a life we once only dreamed of. We are forever in their debt and wish we could name them all here. They wouldn't all fit into one book, however; we'd need volumes.

Instead, we'd like to identify a few individuals whose contributions to this book and our industry are worthy of particular note: Among them: Kelly Olsen, president, Tahitian Noni International; Dave Savula of Pre-Paid Legal Services; Matthew R. Silver, M.D., of FreeLife; Elsa Boynton of Nikken; Mark Yarnell of Legacy for Life; Keith Laggos, publisher of *Money Maker's Monthly*; Kim Klaver, president, Max Out Productions; and Dr. Charles W. King, professor of marketing, University of Illinois at Chicago.

Last, but ever first in our minds, we want to thank Beth Mende Conny, editorial consultant extraordinaire. Beth was in on the project from the outset, helping us organize our thoughts, get the right words onto paper and bring our book to fruition. Her care and high standards pushed us to expand and achieve our goals. We couldn't have done it without her.

Foreword

There are times in life when the student becomes the teacher. This happened to me in 1990.

A major recession had devastated the job market for graduating college students. As a senior professor of marketing at the University of Illinois at Chicago (UIC), I wanted to find a way to help them, so I began researching new career options: starting a business, franchising and direct selling. It was in my analysis of direct selling that I "discovered" network marketing, which I promptly dismissed as a legitimate profession.

A student working on the research project with me asked, "Professor, why are you so negative about network marketing?" I replied, "I'm not being negative, I just don't know anything about it. The Harvard Business School doesn't teach such a thing."

My student persisted. "Why don't I do some additional research — go to the library, study leading companies, attend meetings, interview distributors ... that sort of thing." My response: "I know enough about network marketing to know I don't want to know any more about it!"

He looked at me intently and then said slowly, "Professor, if I gave you that answer, you'd give me an 'F.'" I then looked at him and smiled. "Son, you're right. You just made an 'A.'

Let's study network marketing." Six months later, evidence gathered, I introduced network marketing into the University's marketing curriculum. That was in September 1991.

Since then, I've continued researching and reporting on the industry. I've interviewed more than 10,000 distributors, officers and managers of network marketing companies, leading industry consultants, and trainers and journalists. Although I am not a network marketer myself, I have come to believe in the industry's legitimacy and its strength as a business model. More specifically, I have concluded that:

- Network marketing, through its use of word-of-mouth communication, is the most efficient channel of distribution for moving products and services from the manufacturer or service provider to the end user. (In marketing, this is referred to as speed-to-market.)

- Network marketing not only offers entrepreneurs an alternative career path, but also gives them the leverage (sweat equity) they need to launch a part-time or full-time home-based business.

These conclusions formed the basis of my book *The New Professionals: The Rise of Network Marketing As the Next Major Profession* (Prima Publishing, 2000) and its follow-up, which will be released in 2003. The conclusions also spurred me to found, in 1994, the UIC Certificate Seminar in Network Marketing. Tailored to those wanting to build their organizations, it has become *the* standard for professional education in network marketing. The program has since certified thousands of participants from across the United States, as well as Australia, Canada, Korea, Singapore and Latin America.

In addition to studying the industry, I've taken particular note of what makes for a successful network marketer. Obviously, there are several traits, but one that's always shared is the ability to prospect. That is why I so strongly recommend *Absolutely* Everything *You Need to Know About Network Marketing*. It is a book that delivers on its promise.

Seasoned industry veterans and successful entrepreneurs, Russell and Usa Johnson have written an indispensible step-by-step handbook filled with the cutting-edge techniques that will make you a master prospector. You'll learn how to identify hot prospects, be they down the street, cross-country or overseas. You'll learn how to present your business opportunity most effectively and to build and support a solid downline. You'll also learn how to tap the power of the Internet and that which comes from within, namely, a positive mind-set.

The book is well-organized and easy to read. Its ideas are simple, practical and creative, and demystify a process that new and veteran network marketers alike find challenging. It will undoubtedly become the bible on the subject, for it will help all network marketers reach the upper echelons of their profession.

As an increasing number of individuals build successful network marketing organizations, the industry will gain greater recognition and legitimacy. Through this book, the Johnsons have helped advance the cause of network marketing. For this, we are grateful.

Dr. Charles W. King
Professor of Marketing, University of Illinois at Chicago
Co-founder, UIC Certificate Seminar in Network Marketing

Introduction

You've come to the right place — and book!

Why this book? We think the answer is obvious: To build a wildly successful network marketing business, prospecting is key. Prospecting is not about adopting any one technique, however. Ask the industry's top earners to identify their winning strategies, and they'll quickly note one, two or even 10 or 20. That's because there is no one approach that works for everyone, everywhere, every time. We, like the customers and distributors we recruit, are unique. What works for one of us won't necessarily work for another. And that's great news, for it allows us to expand our prospecting repertoire, and thereby, our opportunities.

In the following pages, you'll discover hundreds of prospecting tips and tools. Some are tried-and-true methods successful network marketers have been using for years. Others are on the cutting edge, allowing you to harness the power of the Internet and the many high-tech tools at your disposal. All work.

Pick and choose as you read. Experiment.

Follow through, and by book's end you'll learn absolutely everything you need to know about prospecting your way to prosperity.

How to use this book

Are you a *new network marketer*? Then we suggest you first skim the book to get the lay of the land, so to speak. We suggest you don't try to absorb everything or try too many techniques at once. Slowly but surely is the way to go. Work through the book chronologically, as each chapter builds on the previous one. Choose two or three strategies you think would be the most effective, given your time, resources and personal style. Commit to adding to your prospecting repertoire weekly. You'll be pleased with the results.

If you are a *veteran network marketer*, skim the book first as well. We know you'll find new techniques and rediscover those that are tried-and-true. As you read, think in terms of your downline. Which tools can you share with them so that they too can build successful businesses?

To assist all of our readers, we've provided previews that outline the contents of each chapter and the many ways to use its information to your advantage. At the end of most chapters, you'll find a section called "Three ways we used these strategies." We've added this material in response to the many inquiries we have gotten to identify techniques we've personally found particularly effective. Our goal is to share all we know and demonstrate the importance of putting your personal stamp on all you do.

As part of that effort, we open the book with our highly personal stories about how we became network marketers. Ours wasn't a straight path. There were more twists, turns and lean times than we care to remember (and that's before we entered the industry!). Still we persevered, and grew stronger and more optimistic each day. For this we have to thank the ultimate secret to our network marketing success. We reveal it in Chapter 8. That's why we suggest that you

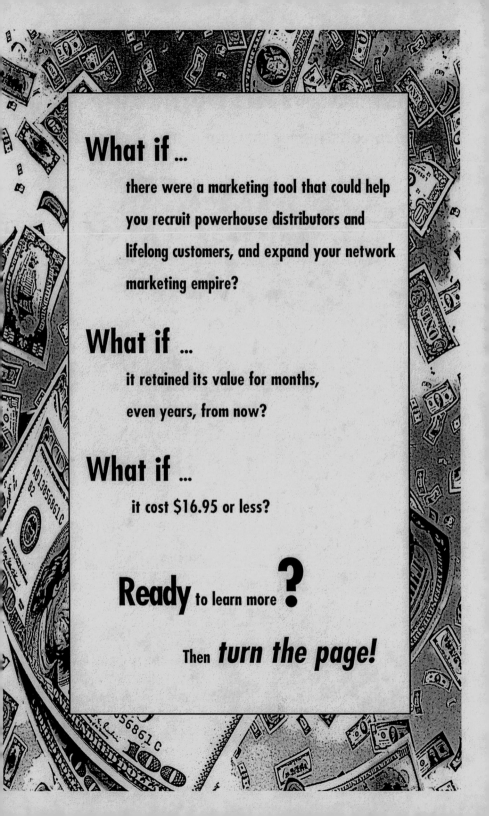

What if ...

there were a marketing tool that could help you recruit powerhouse distributors and lifelong customers, and expand your network marketing empire?

What if ...

it retained its value for months, even years, from now?

What if ...

it cost $16.95 or less?

Ready to learn more **?**

Then *turn the page!*

Network marketing's first and only book
dedicated to turning you into a master prospector.

This book will become the gold standard of network prospecting. The Johnsons have left no stone unturned in their marvelous effort to arm both the novice and seasoned veteran with a tremendous road map to unlimited wealth.
—**Mark Yarnell**, industry leader and author of *Your Best Year in Network Marketing*

Absolutely EVERYTHING
You Need to Know About
Prospecting

The winning strategies today's top earners use to make friends, recruit distributors and build their network marketing empires

Russ Johnson, Ph.D. and Usa Johnson
with Beth Mende Conny

Forward by Dr. Charles W. King
Professor of Marketing, University of Illinois at Chicago, and co-author of
*The New Professionals: The Rise of Network Marketing
As the Next Major Profession*

The book's 208 pages are packed with the hundreds of tips, tools and strategies today's top earners use to build their organizations worldwide. Now you can put yourself in their company.

But don't stop there! Not when you can join the ranks of savvy network marketers and use the book to

- Present your business opportunity in a professional, nonpressured way

- Educate others about how network marketing *really* works and why business pundits claim it is one of the century's hottest industries

- Train your downline to grow their organizations

- Inspire and motivate distributors, customers *and* yourself

---

What the experts are saying:

"Seasoned industry veterans and successful entrepreneurs, Russell and Usa Johnson have written an indispensible step-by-step handbook filled with the cutting-edge techniques that will make you a master prospector ... It will undoubtedly become the bible on the subject, for it will help all network marketers reach the upper echelons of their profession."

—From the forward by Dr. Charles W. King Professor of Marketing, University of Illinois at Chicago

Absolutely EVERYTHING You Need to Know About Prospecting

Here are three ways to take advantage of this great marketing tool.

#1
Order an individual copy for $16.95. (S&H additional)

#2
Order bulk discounted copies. Prices vary based on number of books ordered.

#3 Order customized copies that include any or all of the following
special features:

- Your name on the cover indicating the book is a personalized gift.

- A biographical chapter to introduce prospects to both you and your organization.

- Additional pages profiling your company, its products and the special business opportunities it offers.

Ready to place your order? Need additional information?
Contact:

Biz Builders Consulting, LLC
P.O. Box 1936 • Frederick, MD 21702
T–301/694-9921• F–301/695-3494 •orders@bizbuildersconsulting.com

read and reread that chapter as often as you can. It will change your life as it did ours.

How this book is organized

Part 1 — The tale of two prospectors

Chapter 1. Our Stories

Successful network marketers are made, not born. We're certainly a case in point. Here you'll learn how we came to network marketing from very different places, but shared the same dream: to achieve lifelong prosperity and help others do the same. Prospecting, we quickly learned, was essential to our success.

Part 2—Building your foundation

Chapter 2. Presenting Your Case

When it comes to prospecting, you must be part cheerleader, part business pundit and part corporate executive. The cheerleader in you charges up prospects, the pundit shares data on the industry's incredible growth and the executive introduces your company's stellar products and business opportunity. It's your job to bring all three of your roles together by delivering a strong, finely tuned presentation. You'll learn how to do that here.

Chapter 3. Beyond the Myths

Many prospects have at least one (or two or three) reservations about network marketing. Misconceptions, lack of knowledge about the industry and the unethical practices of disreputable companies — all serve as roadblocks. It's your job to break through them. This chapter will give you step-by-step instructions.

Part 3 — Tried-and-true prospecting techniques

Chapter 4. Prospecting for Gold in Your Own Backyard

You don't need to dig too deep or go too far to find nuggets of gold — namely, great prospects. They're in your own backyard. Here, we'll show you how to identify them through the creation of warm and cold lists. We'll also suggest ways to follow up on your leads.

Chapter 5. Going One-on-one

A list is just a list, unless you work it. That means contacting and meeting with the dozens, perhaps hundreds, of prospects you've identified. Have no fear! There's no mystery or magic to the process if you follow the strategies outlined in this chapter.

Chapter 6. Beyond the One-on-one

When it comes to prospecting techniques, the sky's the limit. Follow your gut and creative urgings. And while you're at it, try the approaches veteran network marketers use to prospect on a larger scale. We'll introduce them to you in this chapter.

Part 4 — Prospecting on the cutting edge

Chapter 7. World Wide Web, Worldwide Reach

Today's network marketer not only prospects one-on-one but one-on-a-million, thanks to that wild and wonderful medium known as the Internet. Web sites, e-books and e-mail are changing the way we do business, and it's our business to stay on the cutting edge. In this chapter, we'll show you how to harness the power of the Internet so you can expand your network marketing empire cross-country and overseas. We'll also introduce you to high-tech/high-touch tools to increase your effectiveness.

Part 5 — Success revealed

Chapter 8.   Our No. 1 Prospecting Tool

This book would not be complete without discussing our No. 1 prospecting tool. We consider it the ultimate key to our success. In this chapter we reveal all so that you too can achieve unparalleled success.

Part 1

The tale of two prospectors

Chapter 1

Our Stories

S uccessful network marketers are not born, they're made. Self-made, that is. We can personally attest to that, which is why we'd like to share our stories with you. As you'll quickly see, we were born into modest circumstances and went through our share of tough times. We didn't bemoan our fate, however. We kept going and growing into a better life.

And what a life it is! We're proud of all we've achieved. More importantly, we're enjoying the fruits of our labor. We planted the seeds of our success not terribly long ago, watered them with faith and effort, and watched them grow. You too can have a plentiful garden. Simply pick up your shovel and work the soil until you too hit pay dirt.

Usa's story

I was born in Bangkok, Thailand, in 1948, into a modest and traditional family. Like other women of my generation, I was expected to marry and raise children. I wanted to do both, yet I wanted more. I wanted an exciting career and great wealth; I wanted to better the lives of others. And that was just for starters! Although

> *Dissatisfaction can be a positive thing if it moves you closer to what you want.*

I longed to share my dreams with others, I knew they'd ridicule me. "Such crazy ideas," I could hear them say. "And from a woman, no less."

Not surprising then, I did what was expected. I married and had a child. Within a few years, however, my life began taking some unexpected turns.

First, after several years of marriage, my husband and I divorced. Although this is hard for any woman, it was particularly hard given the traditional nature of my culture and the fact that I was suddenly thrown into the workforce. Supporting my son, Varong, was my first and only priority. Any dreams I had had while younger were pushed aside. Permanently, I thought.

Luckily, I was able to secure a job as a secretary for the Thai bar association. I say luckily because it not only provided me with the steady income I needed to raise my son, but also created great feelings of dissatisfaction. I, for one, happen to think that dissatisfaction can be a positive thing if it moves you closer to what you want. This is exactly what happened to me. Increasingly, I began to think about what I wanted out of life. Surely, there had to be more than working so many hours for so little pay. But what more was there, and how would I find it? I didn't know the answers, but I had a sense of where to look.

More and more I began dusting off my dreams of wealth and happiness and thinking of starting my life anew, in a place I believed held great promise: the United States. If other immigrants could go there and achieve financial success, so could I. It would take time, it would take effort, but I would at least try.

First, however, I had to deal with the negative responses of others. My family couldn't believe I'd do such a crazy thing. "How will you manage?" they cried. "You've got no money, no place to stay." Even my ex-husband joined in the chorus. "Who do you think you are?" he said. "You'll never be anything more than a secretary." It was difficult to counter their arguments; I was asking the same questions myself.

Nonetheless, I packed my bags, filling them with dreams, fears and photos of my son, whom I left behind in his grandparents' care. "I will return for you as soon as I can make a better life for us," I told him tearfully. Whether it was his wishful heart or unfailing love for his mother, he took my words as a promise. Wanting to prove worthy of his trust, I set off into the great unknown. It was the spring of 1989.

Into the great unknown

America truly was a great unknown. Not only was the culture alien to me, but I spoke little English. What had I gotten myself into?

Upon arrival, I stayed in Las Vegas with a Thai friend who had previously moved to the States. Through her, I found work in California, first as a baby-sitter and then as a restaurant worker. I worked from 11 a.m. to 11 p.m., seven days a week, 52 weeks a year, with only one day off — Christmas. My take-home pay was $200 a week, not even enough to meet my living expenses. It was one of the most difficult and depressing times of my life. Had I really left Thailand for this? At times I thought of swallowing my pride and returning home. But then I'd think about my son, how patiently he was still waiting for me and the better life I had promised. No, I decided. I wouldn't return. Somehow I'd find a better way; somehow I'd get a decent job and life. I'd make my dreams come true.

> *I had rolled some cosmic dice and come up a winner. It all began with a phone call.*

A roll of the dice

In 1991, I moved back to Las Vegas, and it was there that my life took another unexpected turn — this one for the better. It was as if I had rolled some cosmic dice and come up a winner (and what better place to roll the dice than Vegas!). It all began with a phone call.

I was at my friend's house when a man with the most melodious voice called, the kind of voice you hear only on the radio. My friend was out at the time (a fact I tried to explain to the caller in my broken English), and so I took a message. The caller's name was Russell Johnson. Little did I know that I'd be signing my name Usa Johnson within the year.

As it turned out, Russ had a great radio voice because he had been on radio for years. In fact, he had his own business show on American Radio Network. Apparently, my friend had heard a segment Russ did on network marketing (whatever the heck that was!) and contacted him for more information. Upon returning home, my friend immediately called Columbia, Maryland, where Russ lived and worked. They chatted for quite some time, first about network marketing and then ... about me.

Russ, it seemed, had liked the sound of my voice and the person behind the heavy accent. (I guess being in radio allowed him to pick up on things most other folks can't.) I was flattered and flabbergasted. In that one conversation with my friend, Russ learned my short and somewhat sad little story: how I had come to this country in search of a better life and how I had been working horrid jobs under horrid conditions. Russ was sympathetic. He too had been through tough times and his share of low-paying jobs. He admired my spunk and determination to achieve great wealth and happiness. As I would soon learn, he was determined to do the same.

Over the following weeks, my friend and Russ continued to talk. Inevitably, the conversation turned toward me. "How's she doing?" Russ would ask. "Has she gotten her green card yet?" My friend would answer: "She's still struggling, and no, she hasn't gotten her card." Ultimately, Russ thought of a solution to my problems — we could marry.

Russ, it just so happened, was a widower who had been hoping just the right woman would come along. Thinking I might be the one, he suggested I fly out sometime to visit him. If we hit it off, we could marry. And if we didn't … well, we could marry anyway. He wanted me to get a green card and a good shot at life.

To make a long story short, I flew east a few weeks later. We hit it off beautifully and married a few months later. I not only got a wedding band but an unexpected gift: an introduction to the exciting, incredibly profitable world of network marketing.

Prospecting 101

Russ had long been a believer in network marketing, having been in the business some 20-plus years. He had managed to support himself during the last 10 years, but only barely. And yet he persevered. "You've got to try this, Usa," he would say. "Let's work a business together." But I kept putting him off. Me sell anything to anyone? Ha! Marriage might have made my life easier, but it hadn't made me less shy, any braver. "What do you have to lose?" he'd persist. "Do you want to keep working the way you're working now? What kind of future is that for you or us?"

Russ had a point, and an obvious one at that. He was just starting out with a new network marketing company, and while he was fully committed to making it go (as he inevitably did), there was still the initial lean stretch ahead. To make ends meet, I worked days at McDonald's and nights at Taco Bell, making $5 an hour. At the rate I was going, my son would be a senior citizen before I could bring him to the States! I had nothing to lose. I'd give network marketing a try.

Now, if this were a Hollywood movie, I would have become an overnight success. Unfortunately, I was still just me — a former fast-food worker who spoke broken English and was scared silly. And those were my good qualities! Each day it seemed I added yet another item to my shortcomings list. Talk about a negative mind-set.

One of my problems was that I mistakenly believed you had to be a life-of-the-party type who could walk up to a stranger and sign him or her on the spot. That it took me three, four or even 10-plus times to recruit a distributor was dispiriting; that I got so many more nos than yeses was downright devastating.

Russ tried to talk some sense into me. "Success is like a muscle," he'd say. "You've got to build it over time. Besides, getting a whole lot of yeses doesn't mean you've built a strong organization. People who say yes too quickly often give up too quickly.

"And another thing: You don't have to be an extrovert, introvert or an in-betweenvert to make it in this business. Just be yourself. You've got so many prospecting tools at your disposal. Find the ones you're most comfortable with, then grow into others. And don't forget to develop your own. *You* are your greatest asset, Usa. Take stock of your strengths and build on them."

Buoyed by Russ' words, I began to experiment with various prospecting strategies, trying to find the ones that fit best. I quickly realized that some worked better than others in certain settings or among certain types of people.* As obvious as that might sound, it was a revelation: I had been trying to find a one-size-fits-all technique when there was none. That lesson learned, I slowly began

---

* This may sound as if I'm stereotyping, but I'm doing so in a positive way. Retirees, working moms, downsized professionals — all come to network marketing for different reasons. It's my job (and joy), to be responsive to their needs. Although I never make personal assumptions about prospects, I allow myself educated guesses about how their circumstances affect their decisions and shape their dreams.

to build my success muscle.

Not long after that, I had another revelation. I got it in the bathroom, of all places. Actually, I was in the ladies room of a department store. I was at the sink, washing my hands, as was the woman beside me. I don't know what got into

> *Success is like a muscle. You've got to build it over time.*

me that day, but shy little-ole-me gave her a big smile. She smiled back and before I knew it, I was telling her about my business. A week or so later, we met over coffee and I introduced her to my company's products. She became a loyal customer, and a year later, one of my best distributors. What started as a smile turned into a profitable relationship for both of us. Let me tell you, I started smiling a whole lot more after that! But it was easy, never forced. I truly enjoyed people; it was just a matter of letting my enjoyment show. And so I have.

Today, wherever I am, I imagine everyone around me is a good friend. It puts me in a relaxed mind-set and makes it easy to start conversations. I no longer worry about how others will respond to me. There's no need for fear among friends. There's just sharing and caring ... and ready smiles.

A timely introduction

Russ and I began working his business together in 1994. Two years later, we were drawing a six-figure income. My days of flipping burgers and stuffing taco shells were over at last.

That's not the end of my story, however. In 1996 my life took another unexpected turn. Again, it came by way of a phone call.

The call was from a network marketing acquaintance of Russ' who had just become one of the very first distributors for a new and promising company that offered a unique line of health products. Like so many other successful network marketers, this gentleman had worked for several companies over the years, building downlines in the tens of thousands and drawing annual salaries in the six-figures. He obviously knew what it took to make it in the business and how to pick a winning company. That he was willing to put his prodigious energies into this company was a testament to its promise.

Great as the opportunity sounded, however, Russ and I decided not to jump in. We were already committed to our present company and were, at last, seeing the fruits of our labor. Nonetheless, we ordered a sample kit as a courtesy to Russ' friend and to see what the fuss was about. After a few weeks of sampling, I noticed that some of my little aches and pains were gone. Still, I wasn't convinced, and dismissed it as coincidence.

On my own

Right about this time, I was scheduled to visit my son in Thailand. Almost as an afterthought, I brought along the remainder of my samples for friends to try. It was only after their enthusiastic thumbs-up that I began taking a closer look at the company, its products and compensation plan. I liked what I saw.

When I returned to the States, I decided to launch my own business with this new company. Several factors came into play. First, the opportunity seemed like a great one: The company and products were solid, and it would be lucrative and exciting to be among the very first of its distributors. Second, I wanted to test my wings. I had gained so much confidence working with Russ, yet I still wondered if I could make it on my own. There was only one way to find out.

Third, the timing of my launch was right for Russ as well. Although he was still expanding the organization we had built together, he began to devote an increasing amount of time to helping network marketers worldwide achieve success through both tried-and-true and cutting-edge prospecting techniques. Of equal importance, he wanted to spread the word about the promise and legitimacy of network marketing. He had long grown tired of how the industry had been disparaged. He believed it to be a way for people around the world to achieve prosperity, and it was his mission to spread the word.

> *I had gained so much confidence, yet I still wondered if I could make it on my own. There was only one way to find out.*

With these considerations in mind, I set out my own shingle. Using the prospecting techniques that had served me so well in the past and the new ones I was learning each day, I built my business slowly but steadily. I went from four distributors my first month to more than 16,000 two years later. The following year, I had more than 30,000 distributors and was earning an annual income in the mid-six-figures. My American dream had come true.

Proud as I may be of my achievements, however, there are two that mean even more. The first is the charitable organization I founded in my native Thailand. It's called Fuen-Surapee Boonyaparutayus Foundation and is named after my son's grandparents, who had cared so well for him in my absence. Its mission is to help my country's poor and illiterate develop the skills and mind-set they need to create lifelong prosperity.

My second achievement was to bring my son to this country. At last! Varong is in his late 20s now and has become one of my best (and yes, I'll admit, one of my favorite) distributors. He divides his time between the United States, Thailand, Hong Kong, Malaysia and Australia, drawing monthly commissions in the five-figures. Talk about a successful family business! Thank you, network marketing!

But enough about me. Let me turn the stage over to Russ. His story is just as interesting as mine.

Russ' story

I was born in 1935, in Baltimore, Maryland, and as anyone who knows me will tell you, I've always been one to jump into new experiences and make the best of them. For this, I have to thank my parents. My father was a pastor, my mother a homemaker, and they stressed the importance of faith and a positive attitude. I could do anything I wanted in life, they told me, and I believed them.

My parents separated when I was 10. My mother had a hard time making ends meet, so I moved around a bit, living with my aunts, cousins and grandparents, and for a time, in a boys home. I also spent a couple of years with a pastor and his wife who lived on a farm in Virginia. I'd get up at 5 a.m., milk the cows, feed the chickens, chop wood, get a fire going and do whatever else needed to be done. I was a teen then and it wasn't exactly my idea of fun — the farm didn't even have indoor plumbing — but I came out ahead. The experience reaffirmed my faith, helped me develop a strong work ethic and got me in the habit of waking early. (Even today I'm up by dawn to get the most out of each day.)

Off to war

After my stint on the farm, I returned to Baltimore. My mother had remarried by then. My stepfather and I didn't get along particularly well. What was more difficult, however, was that I was held back a grade when I re-entered the city's school system. The Korean War was going on at the time, so I dropped out and enlisted in the Air Force. (The clerk who processed my paperwork apparently didn't care that I was just 16.)

Going into the service, I was given an IQ test and scored better than impressively. My supervisors were surprised as much as I was. I mean, here's this kid who never graduated from high school. Because I had scored particularly well in electronics, I was trained as a control tower operator. The assignment required razor-sharp focus, but I thrived on the challenge. By the time I was 18, I had become a supervisor.

I could do anything I wanted in life, my parents told me, and I believed them.

I was stationed in the States for a while and then shipped off to Japan, where I lived for two years. It was my first exposure to Asian culture — any foreign culture, for that matter — and I was impressed by the quiet dignity of the people and how hard they worked.

The service also was my first exposure to so many educated people. One fellow I knew was a graduate of New York University, a real sharp guy. Back in the barracks, he'd rib me for spending so much of my free time reading pulp fiction. "Why are you wasting your time?" he'd ask. "The world's full of great, important books that will shape your mind." I paid attention to him and began reading up on psychology, sociology, politics, religion — serious topics that gave me a new perspective. I now understood why my father had always pushed me to get a college education. There was a whole world out there and a degree would open the doors to it.

There was one door I had to open first, however. I had to get my high school diploma. Luckily, the service had a GED program. I studied at night and had my diploma in hand by the time I was discharged.

A man of many hats

After leaving the service I was ready to go to college, and thanks to the GI bill, I could.* It took a while to finish up my coursework, however. Fifteen years, to be precise. I left school after my second year. I was married by then and a new dad, and I needed money

---

* First, however, I had to earn *another* GED, this time from the State of Maryland, which required its own diploma before admitting me to college.

> *The way I saw it, people were people. They had the same interests and needs; they all wanted to better their lives.*

coming in, not going out.

During the next decade or so, I took a course here and there and worked lots of different jobs: cab driver, truck driver, bus driver, assembly-line worker, parking attendant, encyclopedia salesman, insurance salesman, janitor ... you name it. When I tell people now about what I was doing then, many shake their heads and say: "Man, you must have hated every minute." But you know, I didn't. As I said, I had a strong work ethic and whatever I was doing, I was going to do well. I also liked meeting people from all walks of life. The way I saw it, people were people. They had the same interests and needs; they all wanted to better their lives. This exposure helped me later when I began prospecting. I felt comfortable talking to just about anyone. It was as if I already knew them.

As you know, the 60s and 70s were a time of great upheaval in our country. You had love-ins, sit-ins, the black power and women's liberation movements, marches against the war and marches for civil rights. I was right in the middle of it, believing, like so many folks back then, that you could effect change through social programs for the underprivileged. Toward that end, I taught in Baltimore's inner city schools. I also was a field supervisor for the Neighborhood Youth Corps and a community organizer for the Urban League. Over time, however, I began to understand that public funds alone couldn't change the way people perceived themselves. If they labeled themselves as disadvantaged, they were going to be disadvantaged; no government program could change that. If they saw themselves as *recipients*, they wouldn't act on their own behalf. What they needed was a different model, one that

would help them achieve self-sufficiency. I would find that model
in network marketing.

A network who?

A number of years later, I was having a beer with a good buddy
at a neighborhood watering hole, when he mentioned a mutual
friend who was now in business for herself and doing quite well.
"What's the business?" I asked. Like so many people outside of
network marketing, he didn't quite understand what it was, let
alone how it worked. Neither did I, but that didn't stop me from
heading over to her place as soon as he and I parted. If someone
was successful in business, I wanted to hear about it. I wasn't
exactly rolling in the bucks, after all.

As it turned out, I arrived at her door in the middle of a home
meeting. Because she was busy, she politely saw me to the door,
promising to call me later. I wasn't so easily dismissed, however. I
asked her to give me some materials, tapes, whatever she had that I
could review in the meantime. I devoured these as soon as I got
home, and was at her door the next day asking for more and to sign
on as a distributor.

This company had its monthly requirements, and I'm not just
talking volume here. I was expected to listen to tapes of its top earners
and to read its inspirational book-of-the-month picks. Hey, no
resistance from me. I had always been an avid reader, only this time,
instead of pulp fiction or heavy-duty texts on heavy-duty subjects, I
tore through books on how to develop a positive mental attitude.

Overnight, I became a student of success. I read biographies of
John D. Rockefeller, Henry Ford, Andrew Carnegie, Henry Kaiser
and hundreds of other business leaders who had built financial
empires and changed the world. I read every book I could find by
the masters of positive thinking: James Allen, Dale Carnegie, Earl
Nightingale, Dr. Norman Vincent Peale and Maxwell Maltz, among

I became a student of success. I read every book I could find by the masters of positive thinking.

others. I listened to self-help tapes as I exercised, drove around town and sat in doctors' offices. I soaked it all up, and yet I wasn't achieving the success I had envisioned.

I didn't get it. Network marketing seemed simple enough — you sold products to people, recruited them to do the same, and before you knew it the bucks rolled in, right?

At first, I told myself it was because I was only working the business part time, but even I didn't buy that after a while. I knew many successful network marketers who had started that way, after all. I also knew some who had launched their businesses while holding down full-time jobs. OK, if that wasn't the problem, what was?

Looking back now, I can see exactly what I was doing wrong. First, I kept jumping from one company to the next, chasing any get-rich scheme I could find. Second, I wasn't choosing the right companies. Some were take-the-money-and-run operations; others looked great on paper but quickly folded; still others had compensation plans that didn't pan out. Third, I was selling products I wasn't excited about. They weren't unique, of high enough quality or priced competitively. Fourth, I often worked more than one company at a time, dissipating my efforts. How could I sing the praises of any one of them if I wasn't working it exclusively?

After 10 years of fumbling, I finally began making enough from network marketing to live on — just barely. Something was still off. It wasn't until Usa came into my life that I set things right.

Themes

If I were writing a traditional autobiography, I'd arrange everything in chronological order. But sometimes chronology doesn't give you the big picture, an accurate sense of who a person is. That's why I'd rather speak in terms of "themes," the constant strands that have shaped my life.

For example, I have always been a spiritual person. My father, like his father, was a pastor. During my impressionable teen years working on a farm, I lived with a pastor. In my 40s, I became a pastor myself. I wanted to serve God and others, to help them reach for the heavens and the best in themselves. Today, I may be more ecumenical in my approach, but my belief has never changed: We have greatness within, and it is our right — our duty — to bring it forth. That's certainly been my goal.

Another theme:

As I mentioned, it took me a while to get my B.A. Nonetheless, I wanted to continue my education, so I went on to earn my master's and Ph.D. All three degrees are in communications, reflecting how much I enjoyed working in radio and TV.

I got my first media job in the early 60s as a part-time disc jockey. I had always thought it would be great to be a D.J., but I hadn't a clue as to how to go about it. Then, one night, I was at a party and met a woman who worked at an FM radio station. She suggested I visit hers and gave me the name of one of the D.J.s. Talk about generous people — this guy not only gave me his time, but let me sit in the studio with him and learn the ropes. I did so for two solid weeks, at the end of which he told the station manager to hire me. The manager just happened to be launching a daily jazz show and needed a host. I jumped at the chance, even though it meant working as an assembly-line worker by day and a D.J. by night. (More precisely, I was on air from midnight to 6 a.m., six days a week.) I had a great time, and played some of the best

> *The more I read, the more my outlook changed. Instead of seeing the impossible, I saw the possible.*

jazz Baltimore had ever heard. Not that anyone was listening, except perhaps my mother (I hope!) and an older woman, a jazz enthusiast who was always calling in requests. Another reason my audience was small was because FM was brand new at the time. Everyone else — and I mean *everyone* else — was listening to AM. FM was considered a doomed experiment. Why, back then, you could buy an FM station for a song (something I sure wish I had done)!

From my first gig on, I had a hand in the media, working full- and part-time in radio and TV, sometimes when holding down other jobs. In addition to being a D.J., I was a talk-show host, a director of special programming for National Public Radio and a TV news anchor and investigative reporter for WBAL-TV 11 in Baltimore. I taught communications at Howard, Antioch and Morgan State universities. I also served as acting general manager for WPFW-Radio, and produced and hosted a nationally syndicated business talk show for American Public Radio.

As much as I liked working in the media, I grew tired and uncomfortable with its primary focus — reporting the news, so much of which was bad. After a while, the negativity got to me. It wasn't that I wanted to bury my hand in the sand; I just didn't want to feel buried by all that could and sometimes did go wrong in the world. That wasn't the kind of world I wanted to live in, and thanks to all the success books I was reading, I knew I didn't have to. The more I read, the more my outlook changed. Instead of seeing the impossible, I saw the possible. And thanks to network marketing, I was meeting a whole lot of people who felt the same. All of us were making a conscious effort to improve our lives and help others do the same. And it was working.

Given my strong belief in the network marketing model, I found as many opportunities as I could to promote the industry. That's how I came to do a segment on it for my syndicated business show — one that caught the ear of a listener in Las Vegas, who just so happened to be a friend of Usa's. (I guess not all news is bad, eh?)

> *All of us were making a conscious effort to improve our lives and help others do the same. And it was working.*

Enter Usa

Usa's already told you about how we met by phone. Hearing her voice, hearing her story — my heart went out to her. I truly wanted to help her. I was also ready to remarry. My wife had passed on seven years earlier. We had been married 27 wonderful years, and I no longer wanted to live alone. When I proposed to Usa, I knew it was a gamble, but I hoped for the best. If we hit it off, great. If we didn't, well we could marry anyway, even if it meant going our separate ways. I knew how much getting a green card meant to her. Happily, we clicked, and in 1992 we tied the knot.

Usa had the quiet dignity and work ethic that had so impressed me while I was stationed in the Far East. Like me, she was determined to achieve great wealth, health and happiness. Unlike me, she wanted nothing to do with network marketing. See, Usa was incredibly shy and absolutely convinced she couldn't sell anything to anyone. I tried to explain that she didn't have to sell as much as share an opportunity, but she wouldn't budge. Eventually, though, she began to entertain the idea.

In 1994, I joined a well-established network marketing company that had just opened its doors in Maryland. I knew I had struck

Working together, Usa and I were an unstoppable team. Our synergy built our business beyond our wildest expectations.

gold. It offered a product line that had no competition. Its training program and compensation plan were great.*

For the first time, I was ready to give 100 percent to building an incredibly wide and deep organization.

That was down the road, however. In the meantime, Usa and I had to make ends meet. She worked at McDonald's by day and Taco Bell by night. This got pretty old, pretty fast, and by force, rather than enthusiasm, she agreed to give network marketing a try. From that point on, our business grew exponentially.

Working together, Usa and I were an unstoppable team. Our synergy built our business beyond our wildest expectations. We gave it our absolute all, putting in long hours, setting ambitious goals and putting in even longer hours. Within a year, we were making $10,000-plus a month. Shy, quiet Usa had become a powerhouse. She could now talk to anyone, anywhere, and in 1996 was ready to go out on her own.

As she mentioned earlier, we got a call that year from a distributor for an up-and-coming company offering a great line of health products. The guy had been in the industry for nearly 20 years, had built downlines of tens of thousands and had earned in the high six-figures. Needless to say, our ears perked up to what he had to say, knowing that if he was involved, the opportunity had to be big. Ultimately, I passed. I was committed to my company and

---

* Although the company had been established nearly a decade earlier, it, like other network marketing companies, ran into the opposition of state officials, who knew little of the industry but were bent on stymying its development. (For more on this narrow mind-set, see Chapter 3, Pages 60–61.)

had learned the hard way that working two businesses wasn't for me. Besides, I was close to retiring from my present company. In other words, I had almost reached the level where I could receive substantial commissions without having to work the business full time. I didn't want to jeopardize that. Usa, however, was ready to test her wings and subsequently signed up.

> *You can't build a business, let alone make it stand, without the cement that holds it all together: a positive mind-set.*

There was another reason I didn't jump in. As a student of success, I wanted to learn more about how the industry's top earners reached the top. What did they know that the rest of us didn't? And so I returned to "school," reading profiles of these individuals in network marketing magazines, books and publications. I also called many of them and asked straight out for their secrets. As you'd expect from network marketers, they were friendly, helpful and enthusiastic. I began compiling all I learned, and before I knew it, I had begun writing this book. Usa soon joined me in the effort, and as we added page after page of tips, we were astounded by the actual number of prospecting strategies network marketers have at their disposal. Our commitment to sharing this information grew stronger every day.

A few last words

When others ask how I became so successful a network marketer, I try to get them to understand that, yes, I've found a few strategies that work particularly well,* but they alone aren't enough. See, you can't build a business, let alone make it stand, without the cement that holds it all together: a positive mind-set. I can't stress that enough.

As far as I'm concerned, this is where too many people go wrong. They just don't believe in their abilities or that the rewards they seek are within reach. They give up inches away; some don't even extend their fingers. Usa and I never gave up, and it is our hope that you will be as stubborn.

Part 2

Building
your foundation

Chapter 2

Presenting Your Case

O ver the years and through our charitable work, we've met many fine individuals who have devoted their lives to raising money for worthy causes and institutions. Ours is a better world because of them. Like network marketers, they hear a lot of nos. Still they persevere, for they know that about 80 percent of the funds they raise will come from a mere handful of individuals or corporations. These major donors make gifts that range from several thousand to several million dollars.

When we ask development officers how they obtain such large gifts, their answer is simple: Present a strong case. That case outlines why a cause is important and how its support will benefit specific groups of people or society as a whole. Just as importantly, that case makes note of the many ways donors themselves can benefit from their charitable contributions (e.g., tax breaks, favorable publicity, a sense of satisfaction and purpose, etc.). Fund-raisers make their case face-to-face over the course of several weeks, months or years. Just one gift, however, can make the effort worth it.

As network marketers, we too must present a solid case if we are to recruit great distributors and loyal customers. We must convey to them the many benefits of becoming part of our organizations and then forming their own downlines. We do this in four ways:

> *Your prospects want to be in the driver's seat, to move forward at their own pace and in their own way.*

1. We let prospects know that network marketing offers a time-tested way of helping them achieve their personal, professional and financial goals.

2. We help them understand the beauty and simplicity of the network marketing model.

3. We introduce them to our company and its stellar record, products and compensation plan.

4. We share the facts and figures that demonstrate why business pundits believe network marketing will be one of the hottest industries in the 21st century.

    Let's step through these points, so you can better present your case.

#1 — Dreams come true

What were your reasons for becoming a network marketer? If you're anything like us and the millions of others in the industry, something specific drew you. That something is drawing others as well.

Your prospects want to be in the driver's seat, to move forward at their own pace and in their own way. They want to control their time and the quality of their lives. Personal satisfaction, professional development and financial reward are all key motivators. No wonder then that network marketing appeals to people of all ages, backgrounds and educational levels. Among your many prospects you will find:

- Entrepreneurs looking for an exciting and challenging business opportunity.

- Successful doctors, lawyers and other professionals seeking new challenges and income streams.

- Stay-at-home moms wanting to supplement their family income.

- Downsized workers determined to take their business lives into their own hands.

- High school and college graduates anxious to jump-start their careers.

- Retirees seeking ways to more fully enjoy their golden years.

- New immigrants wanting to experience the American dream.

- Community-minded individuals seeking ways to help others achieve their dreams.

Note the diverse needs of your prospects. Tap into them, and guaranteed — your prospects will snap to attention. Even if they don't sign up on the spot (let's be realistic here, the vast majority won't), you will at least have planted a seed, one that might well blossom with time.

#2 — An elegantly simple system

No serious prospect will even consider entering the profession without a solid knowledge of how network marketing works. It's not enough, or even accurate, for you to say that the business is a snap. You've got to present a realistic picture of what they can expect so they know what they'll have to do to achieve success. We'd like to help you present this information by outlining what we believe to be the most important "talking points" about network marketing.

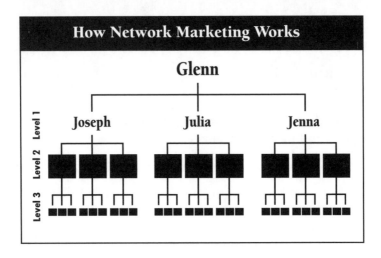

How Network Marketing Works

Glenn

Level 1 — Joseph   Julia   Jenna

Level 2

Level 3

Network marketing defined

Explain to your prospects that network marketing is a system for marketing and distributing goods and services. These goods and services can be anything and everything: makeup, nutritional products, water filter systems, pet products, vacuum cleaners, computers, long distance telephone services, legal services ... the list goes on and on.

Point out that network marketing companies are no different from other companies in that they both provide consumers with what they want and need. Where they do differ, however, is in their business structure.

As your prospects may or may not know, network marketing companies don't have to go through a bunch of middlemen to get their products into the hands of customers. Rather, these companies produce, market and distribute their goods directly to the end-users through distributors.

Distributors are independent company representatives. They get a commission on every sale made. The more sales they make, the greater their profits.

What distributors do

Explaining the role of distributors is an essential part of your presentation. How else can prospects understand where and how they fit into an organization? To distributors like us, the concept is remarkably simple, yet it can be tricky to explain. That's why we suggest you use a visual aid, such as the one on Page 48.

Via the graphic, have your prospects meet Glenn, who, like them, is new to the business. As you'll explain, Glenn not only sells his company's products but recruits three other individuals who work the business as he does. Together, Joseph, Julia and Jenna form Glenn's first level or line. Glenn gets a commission on all the sales he personally makes *and* on all the sales his first line makes.

As Glenn's first line works the business, they not only sell their company's products but recruit their own distributors, forming their own first lines (Level 2 in the graphic). Like Glenn, these distributors get a commission on the sales they and their respective first-line distributors make. Glenn, in the meantime, does even better. He will not only get a commission on all of his own sales but also on the sales of his Levels 2, 3, 4, etc. As your prospects will quickly see, this can be very profitable for Glenn — and them.

When presenting this information, it's important to note that the visual is simplistic and that different network marketing companies have somewhat different commission structures. Nonetheless, the basic concept crosses all lines and illustrates how they can build an organization from the top down and rather quickly.

Additional benefits

Don't stop your presentation yet! There are other great points to make. For example:

- **Glenn is in business for himself.** Although he is a distributor for a particular company, he is not one of its employees. Rather, he is an independent contractor who sets his own hours and grows his business at his own pace.

- **Glenn's financial outlay is minimal.** He doesn't need vast sums of money to launch his venture. In fact, like most network marketers, he will probably need just a couple hundred dollars or so to get started.

- **Glenn doesn't have to reinvent the wheel or go it alone.** The company Glenn represents, like all legitimate network marketing companies, will have created a precise blueprint of success for him to follow. This blueprint covers all company policies and procedures, and includes all of the materials Glenn will ever need: products, promotional materials, stationery and everything in-between.

- **Glenn will have a sponsor** (a mentor) to show him how to build his business step-by-step. His sponsor will be part coach, cheerleader, colleague and friend.

- **There are no prerequisites to Glenn's success.** He is fine as is and ready as is. He doesn't need to be a college graduate or even a high school graduate. He doesn't need to have specialized training or previous work experience. He doesn't need to be a certain age or sex, or come from a certain socioeconomic group or locale. In this respect, network marketing is the great equalizer. It creates a level playing field for anyone who enters the field. No other industry or profession is so democratic.

#3 — A stellar company

We believe that becoming a network marketer is a great decision *if* you choose the right company. The right company offers a compensation plan that is generous and easy to understand, and products that are unique and of high quality. The company should also have a compelling vision, seasoned management and cutting-edge distributor and customer support. That's a tall order, but one prospects expect to have filled. As a company representative, it's your job to do the filling. Here are some pointers that will be of help.

Share your excitement

Your prospects need to know that network marketing companies are not all alike. Some are more successful, dynamic and focused than others. Yours is one of them, so sing its praises in your presentation. Don't exaggerate or make false promises. If your company's all you say it is, there's no need to. Further, prospects have a sixth sense for recognizing a con job.

Introduce your company's products

Most prospects understand that network marketing companies differ, as do the products they offer. Vitamins from one company, for example, are not interchangeable with vitamins from another. It's up to you to explain the differences and the many reasons why your offerings are superior. Perhaps it's the ingredients or pricing. If the market for your products is expanding, mention this as well.

Introduce your company's management

No offense, but prospects need to know that there's more to your company than you. Tell them they are joining an organization of thousands (perhaps millions worldwide) and that an seasoned, visionary team is at the helm.

Through promotional materials and the company's Web site, introduce prospects to your founders and/or CEO, chief financial and operations officers, managers of operations, and distribution and administrative personnel. Among these individuals, your prospects will be getting decades of network marketing experience. A good selling point, therefore, is that prospects will be in good hands.

Introduce your company's compensation plan

Stairstep, Breakaway, Matrix, Unilevel and their hybrids* are just

---

* To learn about these and other plans, refer to *Direct Sales: An Overview* by Keith Laggos, Ph.D., MBA, publisher of *Money Maker's Monthly*. It's an excellent resource covering all aspects of our industry.

some of the compensation plans today's network marketing companies offer*. Most prospects don't want a detailed explanation of the pros and cons of each (although you should be familiar with them, should a prospect ask). Rather, they will want to know about *your* company's plan. Be prepared to discuss it in-depth.

That said, our experience shows that prospects are most interested in how the commission structure and bonus systems work, what their potential profits might be and how quickly they can draw an income. A strong presentation will touch upon these issues without hype or overly ambitious projections.

Introduce your company's distributor and customer support system

Your prospects are busy people. They don't have time to waste. It's your job to let them know how your company oversees the countless details that plague most business start-ups. Be specific, mentioning things like the following:

- Inventory
- Placement and shipment of orders
- Tracking of sales, bonuses and commissions
- Design and production of forms, promotional and training materials, stationery
- Creation and hosting of Web sites
- Ongoing training, research and development

#4 — A revolutionary industry*

Pick up any newspaper, magazine or book that objectively reports on the network marketing industry, and you'll quickly see why business

---

* Our thanks to Dr. Charles W. King, who provided updated information and analysis for this section. King, an industry expert and senior professor of marketing at the University of Illinois at Chicago, is the author of *The New Professionals: The Rise of Network Marketing As the Next Major Profession* (Prima Publishing, 2000). His follow-up book will be released in 2003.

pundits claim that network marketing will be one of the hottest opportunities of the 21st century (as if we didn't know!). The data is impressive, so why not share it with your prospects. Here are just some of the many facts we think they should know:

- *More than $82 billion worth of goods and services were sold through network marketing in 2000, about $26 billion of that in the United States alone.* In 1991, the U.S. figure was just under $13 billion. This means network marketing sales doubled between 1991 and 2000. These are big numbers, and they're going to get bigger. In fact, some experts believe that network marketing will account for one-third of all goods and services sold in Western countries within the next few years.

- *The global market is expanding and so too is the influence of network marketing.* The vast majority of the world's population — 94 percent — lives outside the United States. Amazing as that may be, it's even more so when you think of what that might mean for you, as a network marketer. Thanks to the wonders of the Internet and other technological innovations and the forward-thinking management of some of the hottest network marketing companies today, there are no such things as international borders. In fact, many network marketing companies have extended their reach around the world. Quixtar, Morinda and Nu Skin are each in 30-plus countries. Quixtar, in fact, makes the majority of its sales overseas. Name a solid network marketing company today, and you'll find it crosses international borders.

- *On a global basis, the number of network marketers grew more than 242 percent between 1991 and 2000.* In the United States during that time period, the number of network marketers increased more than 100 percent, from 5.1 million to 11 million.

- *Fourteen countries account for about 90 percent of all worldwide sales.* These countries, in order of sales, are: the United States, Japan, Mexico, Korea, France, Germany, Brazil, the United Kingdom, Italy, Australia, Taiwan, Argentina, Canada and Venezuela. Japan and the United States together account for about 62 percent of total sales.

- *Network marketing companies are moving into the commercial mainstream and are actively traded on NASDAQ and the New York and American stock exchanges.* Among them: Amway, Avon, Excel Telecommunications, Nu Skin, Pre-Paid Legal Services and Tupperware.

- *Traditional companies are moving into network marketing* in an effort to reach consumers without incurring the costs of employing a full-time sales force or conducting national advertising campaigns. These companies have adopted network marketing techniques, formed alliances with network marketing companies and/or bought network marketing companies themselves (and made huge profits on them), all since the 1970s. They include, among others: Fuller Brush, Gillette, Colgate-Palmolive, MCI, Sprint, AT&T, Rexall, Citigroup, Teleglobe and Procter & Gamble.

- *Business leaders are embracing the network marketing model.* For example, Robert T. Kiyosaki, multimillionaire and best-selling author of *Rich Dad/Poor Dad* (Warner Books, 2000), is one of numerous business leaders who believes network marketing is one of the quickest, easiest and most affordable ways to move into what he calls the "B quadrant."

  All of us, Kiyosaki states, fall into one of four quadrants of wealth: "E" (employees), "S" (self-employed or small business owners), "B" (large business owners) or "I" (investors).

Employees, he says, earn only what their employers will pay; the self-employed earn only what they can generate. Large business owners, by contrast, sustain and expand their businesses through the efforts of others. This allows them, like "I"s, to invest their profits in financial opportunities that lead to even greater profits and long-term wealth.

According to Kiyosaki, the best route to the "I" quadrant is through the "B" quadrant, which is where network marketing comes in. For minimal investment, an average person in the "E" or "S" quadrants can build a strong "B" quadrant business.

"The network marketing system and the industry [have] done a great service by literally leveling the playing field," Kiyosaki notes. "They did this by making the opportunity for truly great wealth available to anyone willing to follow the system and enter the world of the B quadrant ... the quadrant of the very rich."

In closing

As we believe we've demonstrated in this chapter, presenting a case for network marketing and your company is important — and easy. There's much to share, all of it informative and exciting. But alas, you have to go beyond the sharing. You also have to anticipate and respond to the misconceptions your prospects may have of the network marketing model. Have no fear. We'll walk you through the process in Chapter 3, *Beyond the Myths*.

Three ways we've used this information

1. Right off, we knew we had to develop a compelling presentation to help prospects envision success, however defined. Actually, the two of us developed scores of presentations because we knew no one of them would appeal to all individuals or highlight our respective strengths. For example, successful professionals would likely want to hear about new income streams, while working moms might be more interested in home-based business opportunities.

Once we had our presentations blocked out, we fine-tuned them by rating our performance after each one-on-one or home meeting. (That's how our Performance Evaluation table on Page 123 came into being.) We're still fine-tuning our presentations as we expand our organization overseas and in different cultures, and incorporate it into teleconferences, interactive Web-based programs, etc.

2. Because the majority of all prospects are new to network marketing, we always incorporate as many visual aids in our presentations as possible. In addition to the type of chart found on Page 48, we include everything and anything our companies offer. They're attractively and professionally produced, and present the information as it relates to the specific business opportunity. We suggest you do the same.

One other visual we've found effective: photocopies of our first-year commission checks. In our case, they demonstrate how with commitment (and quite a few long hours), our income increased monthly.

3. Never has there been such a great time to become a network marketer. Our industry is growing exponentially, here and abroad, making it one of the hottest business opportunities of the 21st century. What a selling point! That's why we share this information every chance we get. Incorporate that into your presentations as well.

We also recommend that you keep current on industry developments. To do so, visit the Direct Selling Association (DSA) Web site (www.DSA.org). DSA tracks data on both our profession and individual companies. The World Federation of Direct Selling Associations offers the same type of information, but for companies outside the United States. Its Web site is www.wfdsa.org.

We're not content to stop there, however. We want to stay abreast of developments beyond network marketing that may affect the types of individuals we prospect and how we approach them. To illustrate, here are some items we recently came across:

■ According to year 2000 U.S. Census Bureau findings, new immigrants now account for half of the new wage earners who are joining the workforce. When we read this in a front-page story in *The Washington Post*, we immediately thought of how many of these immigrants might not have the language skills, professional skills and/or education to find gainful employment. Network marketing may be the vehicle they need to not just survive, but thrive.

■ According to another newspaper story, this time from *The Frederick News Post*: The "labor force participation rate" for older workers is increasing, meaning seniors, increasingly, are opting not to retire. Certainly, poor stock returns and misdirected 401(k) funds play a role, but there are other reasons. Today's older Americans are living longer and have a healthier lifestyle. Many are not content to stay at home; they're seeking new experiences and challenges. Network marketing may be just the ticket.

■ And one more article, this one from the December 2002 issue of *Entrepreneur*, whose cover story listed the hottest industries, trends and markets in the year(s) to come. Among the markets we found listed: singles, sleep-deprived individuals, middle-aged women and overweight people. How might your products meet the needs of these prospects?

As we've shown, everywhere you look — be it in the newspapers, magazines or on the radio or TV — you'll find information that you can file away or put to immediate use. Any one piece can help strengthen your presentation; all can help you better understand the many reasons why our industry's time has come.

Chapter 3

Beyond the Myths

Not everyone knows a great thing when they see it. Some people need to see it again, and again. Perhaps they think it's too good to be true or that they're not good enough for *it*. Whatever the case, these individuals need to be reassured and educated.

Prospects are the same way. Sure, you'll have some interested in network marketing in general, and your company in particular. Most, however, will be cautious, even skeptical. But that's OK, for it gives you a unique opportunity to talk about the key points discussed in Chapter 2, "Presenting Your Case." You want your prospects to make well-informed decisions. Our experience shows that those who jump into the business blindly are the very ones who jump back out. That's no way to build an empire.

As a distributor, you must be ready to respond to your prospects' concerns and counter any misconceptions they may have. That's why this chapter is so important. We want you to have the ammunition you need to meet objections head on. Generally, these objections can be grouped into what we call the "seven myths of network marketing." We'll explore each one in the pages that follow.

Myth #1

Network marketing is a pyramid scheme

This is one of the most common and inaccurate myths of all. One of your first orders of business, therefore, will be to draw a distinction between network marketing and pyramids.

Your prospects need to know that pyramid schemes are illegal. Some of these pyramids (also known as Ponzi schemes) sell products and services at prices inflated beyond imagination. One gets little, if anything, in return. Other pyramids profit by requiring "distributors" to buy huge inventories of nonreturnable products, in addition to purchasing expensive training tapes and manuals. Still others require distributors to pay a one-time fee in exchange for "unlimited" residual income. How does one get this income? By signing up others, who then sign up others, etc. No goods or services are exchanged, only empty promises of overnight wealth. It's no surprise then that the only ones getting rich are the fly-by-night companies offering these "once-in-a-lifetime" deals.

Legitimate network marketing companies, by contrast, offer quality goods and services at reasonable prices. These offerings are at the very heart of their business. In fact, they *are* the business. You don't have to be a distributor to purchase them, although you can opt to do so. Many individuals, in fact, take this route because it lets them buy products wholesale. They can then sell them retail and/or build a business by helping others do the same.

Here's another distinguishing feature of network marketing companies that's worth noting: The success of any one company is predicated on the success of its distributors. Accordingly, it's in the company's best interests to retain distributors. It does this by offering top-notch training, state-of-the-art administrative support, a generous compensation plan and a variety of incentives. Prospects would be hard-pressed to find a pyramid company that does the same.

So far so good by way of explanation, but don't pat yourself on the back just yet. Sharp prospects will want to know why, despite the differences between

Thanks to public education and the growing ranks of network marketers, our time is coming.

pyramids and legitimate network marketing, misconceptions abound. Your response: Pyramid schemes past and present continue to cast a shadow over the industry. In addition, federal and state regulators have been slow (and some would say unable) to distinguish between the two. The industry as a whole and individual companies in particular have had to fight for regulatory acceptance. For example, although network marketing is 50-plus years old, it wasn't until 1979 that the Federal Trade Commission ruled that Amway, an industry pioneer and stalwart, was not a pyramid. No wonder acceptance of the network marketing industry has been so slow in coming. Thanks to public education and the growing ranks of network marketers, however, our time is coming. In fact, some say it's already here.

Myth #2
No one gets rich in network marketing

Another falsehood. The industry is full of rags-to-riches stories and individuals who earn six- and seven-figure incomes. We should know — we're among them. The industry is also full of what we call nice-clothes-to-riches stories, namely individuals who have left decent jobs and salaries behind to achieve greater wealth and independence. All prospects want to know if they will be among either of these ranks. The answer: It's up to you. If you work hard and persevere, you can make it.

Nonetheless, we must share a shocking fact with your prospects as well: Only 5 percent of all network marketers reach the upper echelons, and typically after some 10 years in the business. Ninety percent drop out by the end of their second year. Undoubtedly, your prospects will want to know what separates the top earners from the vast majority of others. So tell them:

- **_Wildly successful marketers are deeply committed_** to the network marketing model and fully committed to their respective companies. The majority of these individuals work with one company only, concentrating, rather than dissipating, their energies.

- **_They choose their companies wisely._** They've learned how to spot a solid, dynamic company. It's a skill they've learned over time. Many successful network marketers (including us) have cycled through three to four companies before settling on the one that works best for them. Their previous companies might not have offered a generous enough compensation plan, or a product or service they could truly stand behind. Others might not have had strong enough management or a solid business plan. Others might even have gone belly up, taking downlines with them. Rather than bemoaning their fate, however, these top distributors used their hard-earned knowledge to make better choices. Many also signed with newly launched companies, allowing them to be among the first levels of distributors.

Myth #2 continues on Page 66

How to choose a network marketing company

No matter how great your presentation may be, individuals new to network marketing (and some veterans as well) will be wary of getting involved with a company they know little about. That's as it should be, which is why it's important to encourage prospects to look closely at the following.

The company's business practices. Suggest that prospects contact the Better Business Bureau (www.bbb.com) and the Federal Trade Commission (www.ftc.gov) to see if any complaints have been lodged against the company. They might also want to contact their state attorney general's office. Tell them to search the Web for information about the company. They likely will find hundreds, even thousands, of links, but if they glance through a few pages worth of search results, they might find a newspaper or magazine article that provides information not found in the company's materials.

The company's products. Stress the importance of falling in love with a company's offerings. Tell prospects to try its product line *over an extended period of time*, and to give samples to family and friends for their opinions.

The company's potential market. Help prospects understand that a company's product line must have market appeal *and* potential. Put another way, it must be something people want *now*, and that an increasing number of them will want *later*, be it months or years down the road. Flash-in-the-pan products are made by flash-in-the-pan companies, the very kind prospects should avoid.

Assessing appeal and potential is far from an exact science. However, prospects can get some of this information from a company's promotional materials. Tell them to look carefully at how a company positions itself in the worldwide market and at the types of products it will soon add to its line. This information will tell them a lot about a company's vision.

Suggest that they do additional reading. For example, if they're thinking of joining a company that produces a line of vitamins specially designed for individuals 50 years or older, prospects should research whether this age group is increasing and the types of health issues they face. Would vitamins be of benefit to them? Another example: If prospects are thinking of joining a company that provides phone services, they should familiarize themselves with the present state of the telecommunications industry. Their readings will reveal which services are hot and which are not.

The company's executives, upliners, downliners and customers. Just as prospects wouldn't take a job without meeting their prospective employers, they should not sign with a company without knowing at least something about its executives. Executives are like ship captains; it is their responsibility to guide their companies and explore new lands. Prospects must learn all they can about these individuals through the company's promotional materials and Web site, both of which feature profiles. (Or *should.* Companies that offer little background information may well have inexperienced executives at the helm.) Prospects should look at depth of experience and vision specifically. Where do they see their company heading? What are its sales projections? How has the company performed since its launch? Is its growth upward, downward or flat? How many distributors do they have now and how will these numbers grow?

Prospects should also talk to upliners and downliners to assess the extent to which a company fulfills its promises. Upliners need not be direct sponsors, however. They can, for example, be among the company's very first line of distributors. Reassure prospects that these individuals will be more than happy to speak with them. Ours is a people business, after all, and the goal of all sponsors is to help others succeed.

When talking with upliners, have them forward the names of their top distributors. Prospects should then chat with these individuals to get a firsthand look at how the company operates and how good its compensation plan really is. Distributors can also share how effective company training programs and sponsor support are.

Finally, have prospects talk to customers. What is it they like most about the company's products? Are orders handled simply and efficiently?

The company's Internet presence. This might not have been a consideration five years ago, but it's essential today. At the very least, prospects should expect a company to have a Web site, and a darn good one. A great site serves as an interactive storefront, reference desk, training and fulfillment center, and gathering place for distributors. Great sites also make it easy for prospects to get commissions on all sales that come across the Internet. Companies with amateurish, difficult-to-surf sites may well be companies prospects should avoid.

Myth #2 continued from Page 62

- **_They are realistic._** They know, from experience, that they must put in long hours in the short-term to enjoy substantial residual income in the long-term. They also know that their most important role is not so much recruitment as retention. In other words, they become dynamic leaders who use vision, smarts and generosity of spirit to help others reach their personal and financial goals.

- **_They are believers._** They believe in network marketing. They believe in their company. They believe in those they sponsor. They believe in hard work and persistence. And they believe in themselves. Original thinkers, they don't go along with the adage, "Seeing is believing." They know that "believing is seeing," and they can see for miles! They know there is enough wealth for everyone and they're determined to enjoy their share.

Myth #3

It takes money to make money

Yes, it does, and don't let your prospects think otherwise. Any and all network marketing companies have a start-up fee that allows distributors to come into the business at the ground level. The fees themselves can range from $25–$1,000-plus. We believe that's reasonable, even cheap, considering the start-up fees for franchises. To prove it, show your prospects the sidebar on the next page. Impressed as they may be, be prepared for the two questions that will almost always follow: What's the catch? What are the hidden costs?

Assure them that there is no catch; there are no hidden costs. Everything truly is laid out in black and white. Prospects do need to know, however, that there's a reason why the word "start" is in "start-up." It indicates a beginning, an entry point. The initial fee

Does It Take Money to Make Money?

It sure does if you decide to buy a franchise. Consider the approximate start-up costs of the following companies. (Note: This information was obtained in 2003 via Web sites and direct calls. Dollar amounts have been rounded out.)

Athlete's Foot	$201,000–$640,000
Blockbuster	$325,000–$700,000
Denny's	$901,000–$1,700,000
GNC	$132,000–$182,000
Gold's Gym	$300,000–$2,000,000
Jenny Craig	$150,000–$500,000
KFC	$1,000,000–$1,700,000
McDonald's	$489,000–$1,500,000
Subway	$52,000–$191,000
Supercuts	$90,000–$164,000

Now consider the approximate start-up costs for the following network marketing companies:*

Quixtar	$39–$150
Excel	$245
FreeLife	$29
Herbalife	$49–$75
Legacy for Life	$50–$350
Morinda	$140
Nu Skin	$25
Pre-Paid Legal	$149–$249
USANA	$49–$300

* Start-up costs are just that—initial fees, much like membership fees, that are paid to the company. See pages 66 and 68.

Expected costs

The costs below are in addition to a company's start-up fees and product costs. This list is not exhaustive, and not all of the items on it are required.

- Telephone

- Answering machine or service

- Internet access, e-mail account

- Promotional materials

- Photocopying

- Stamps

- Fliers

- Ads

- Refreshments (for home meetings)

- Hall rentals (for large-scale opportunity meetings)

- Mileage

- Travel and hotel (for statewide and regional meetings, company conventions, etc.)

they pay is much like a membership fee. For it, they will generally get a package that introduces the company, its products, commission structure, etc. This will be laid out in one, several or all of the following: detailed booklets, brochures, tapes, videos and product samples. It's up to prospects to decide what they want to do next. For example:

- They can opt to purchase products wholesale for their own use.

- They can opt to purchase products wholesale and then retail them to family, friends, etc.

- They can opt to do both of the above *and* become distributors. This enables them to build their own businesses and recruit other distributors, who do the same. They then earn commissions from both their downline and their distributors' downlines (as outlined in the graphic on Page 48).

Are there costs beyond start-up fees? Of course. Tell prospects it's much like owning a clothing store. The suits and dresses don't come free, but each can be purchased at reduced rates that enable prospects to make a profit and expand their business.

These costs, coupled with those shown to the left, are part of doing business as a network marketer. However, have them note the expenses they would *not* have to assume, as would clothing stores and most other businesses. For example:

- They wouldn't have to carry an inventory of goods; they'd order the quantities they wanted, when they wanted them.

- They wouldn't have to track their sales or commissions; their company will do that for them.

- They wouldn't have to design or produce stationery, brochures, Web sites, etc. Again, their company will do all that, plus provide them with ongoing training and support.

All of these and more are included in the cost of doing business. Not a bad deal, we'd say.

Myth #4

There's no such thing as an overnight success

We agree. Our experience has shown that it takes a whole lot of nights to become an overnight success. The network marketing model may be simple, but that doesn't mean any of us achieve success in a night, week, month or even a year. We certainly didn't. Rather, we worked long and hard for it. There wasn't a day when we didn't make at least a couple of prospecting calls. There wasn't a week when we didn't host, or help others host, a home meeting. Even now we keep working to build our business, though we do it part time ... most of the time, that is. Some months we work 12-hour days, not including the time Usa spends in Thailand, her native country, where she's spreading the word about network marketing and supporting her growing downline.

Most major network marketing companies are expanding their reach overseas as well, opening new markets in Europe, South America, Asia and beyond. They know that in today's global economy there are no boundaries, only unlimited opportunities for distributors. We want to be in on the action, which means we will be putting in some even longer hours. We know, as your prospects will learn, that this is time well spent.

Myth #5

You need a downline of thousands to make money

Distributors who stick with network marketing will one day have a downline of thousands. As you'll inform your prospects, it's part of the business model and one of the most exciting things about the industry. Imagine: They can work their own hours, all from home, and you can have a workforce of many dedicated individuals.

Nonetheless, your prospects should know they don't need *all* of these people to achieve success. All they need are one to three individuals. Undoubtedly, they will ask how this could be. Respond by showing them the graphic at right.

Glenn (remember him from Chapter 2?) recruits Joseph, Julia and Jenna as his first line, or level. They, in turn, recruit their own first lines, who recruit their own first lines, etc. The deeper and wider Glenn's organization, the greater his commissions.

Distributors, however, are not all cut from the same mold. Some

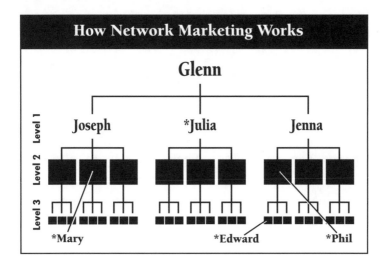

How Network Marketing Works

will work full time, others part time. Some will be fully committed, others will not. Some will want to build a downline of thousands, others will only want to buy products wholesale. As you can imagine then, some distributors generate more income than others.

Glenn knows this all too well. Julia, on his first level, gives the business her all. Joseph and Jenna do not. Does that mean Julia's downline will generate more income? Not necessarily.

Have prospects take a closer look at Joseph's first line. There they'll find Mary, a real go-getter. She builds an organization that's wider and deeper than any other distributor at her level. Her efforts pay off, not only for her, but also for her upline, more specifically, Joseph and Glenn.

The same can be said of Edward. He's in Phil's front line and on a fast track to build his business. He sells more products and recruits more distributors than anyone in his upline. Nonetheless, his upline — Phil, Jenna and Glenn — share in his success.

What does this all mean to your prospects? Simply that they only need one to three distributors, whatever their level, to realize their personal and financial goals. They need not recruit thousands to achieve the same result.

Myth #6

You've got to strong-arm people into signing up

Absolutely not! In fact, you must tell your prospects that doing so will have the opposite effect. They'll wind up recruiting people who joined only because they felt pressured to. The vast majority of these individuals will drop out by the end of their third week — and they'll blame their sponsors for their failure.

Accordingly, let prospects know that the soft sell is the best sell. It's the *only* sell. There's no need to strong-arm anyone. If you love your company and its products and services, if you believe in network marketing and all that it offers, you don't have to convince anyone of anything — you merely have to share what you believe to be a winning business opportunity. Not everyone will hear the call. Concentrate your efforts on those who do. Most prospects will understand — and be relieved — by this.

Myth #7
You need to be a natural-born salesperson

How untrue! Just ask people who know the two of us, especially Lisa. They'll tell you she's the shy, quiet type — and they're right. She still finds it hard to talk in front of groups of people, be they small or large. But what she may lack in courage, she makes up for in belief. She believes in network marketing, her company's products, her downline ... and just as importantly, herself. Her sincerity shines through; it's what helped her grow her business.

Your prospects need to know that there are hundreds of thousands, maybe millions, of network marketers out there like her. We've recruited quite a few of them ourselves, and continue to be amazed at how effective the "strong, silent types" can be. Their contributions prove that network marketing truly is the great equalizer — not just financially, but personally. It allows people of all races, creeds, colors and backgrounds to achieve success — just as it allows people of various personality types to realize their dreams.

Three ways we've used these strategies

1. It's difficult to sing the praises of the network marketing industry in general, and our companies in particular, when myths about the industry abound. Nonetheless, as is our practice, we see the upside in all of this. If nothing else, the myths have strengthened our resolve. They have made us more determined than ever to change the industry's image and take every opportunity we can to sing its praises. Ours is more than a legitimate industry. It is a model by which traditional companies are expanding their businesses. It is one of the hottest businesses of the 21st century, and a model by which traditional companies are expanding their reach and increasing their profits. More importantly perhaps, it's a way to help people of all races, creeds and colors, and all economic, social and educational levels, achieve lifelong prosperity.

2. Another upside of the myths: They make it easier to deal with the inevitable nos we get from prospects. We know that it's not personal. Rather, in great part it's a response to misinformation. We stress this to our downline, and it has made it easier for so many of them to prospect with greater confidence and savvy. Their presentations are sharper and more effective because they address the myths even before they are raised.

3. Of all the misconceptions others have of our industry, the most difficult, even heartbreaking, to deal with is the one about overnight success. Although so many prospects say they don't believe it, they expect it nonetheless, thanks in no small part to unethical distributors desperate for the same success. To see their hopes dashed can have long-term consequences for some. They feel burned, or that they've failed. They become embittered, convinced that the successful network marketers they see have performed some slight of hand.

This truly bothers us, which is why we go out of our way, and then some, to paint a real picture of what it takes to build a business. We share our stories, just as we shared ours with you in Chapter 1. We help them understand what it takes to build and sustain an organization of our size. We burst their bubbles, so to speak, replacing them with realistic goals and milestones and a multidimensional understanding of prosperity. Only some will understand that success is a balance of personal, professional and economic achievement. The prospects who grasp this become stellar distributors. Those who don't, well, they will have to learn the hard way.

Part 3

Tried-and-true prospecting techniques

Chapter 4

Prospecting for Gold in Your Own Backyard*

W hen gold was discovered in 1848, tens of thousands flocked to California's Sierra Nevada Mountains to make it rich. Only a small number did so. The vast majority thought that all they had to do was grab a pan, step into a river and sift through dirt. They were right, but only in part. What they didn't grasp was that they had to stick with it, not just for a day or two, but for weeks, months, perhaps even years. Not surprisingly, many gave up and moved on to the next get-rich-quick scheme.

You can learn two important lessons here. One, short of winning the lottery, wealth does not come overnight. It takes persistence and belief. Two, unlike gold mining, you don't need to find a lot of gold to achieve wealth; you just need a few nuggets, namely two to three committed distributors, to build a highly successful business. In this chapter, you'll learn how to find them.

---

* When we say backyard, we mean your immediate community, be it your neighborhood, city or circle of family, friends and colleagues. In Chapters 7 and 8, we'll focus on prospecting on a broader scale.

Step #1
Take note

Before you dash out the door, company packets in hand, let's talk about what prospecting is and what it is not. Understanding the difference will help you better focus your efforts.

- Prospecting is not about promising the moon — quick and easy cash — or strong-arming anyone into becoming a distributor. It's about helping others build their own businesses over time and through hard work.

- Prospecting is not about becoming a slick salesperson and wowing everyone you meet. It's about communicating authentically, according to your own style.

- Prospecting is not about making hundreds of phone calls a week to everybody and anybody you can think of. It's about identifying those individuals who would be most receptive to your offering and introducing them to your products or business opportunity.

- Prospecting is not about recruiting others, then racing off to recruit yet more. It's about relationship-building and nurturing your downline, so its members can build strong downlines of their own.

- Prospecting is not about occasional efforts. It's about consistency and an infectious enthusiasm that catches the attention of others.

- Finally, prospecting is not mere busy work. It's the one activity, when sustained, that guarantees your network marketing success.

Step #2
Do your homework

In network marketing, excitement is the currency by which products and business opportunities are sold. If you feel ho-hum about your company and its offerings, how can you expect to attract others into the fold? Enthusiasm begins with familiarity. That means knowing your product line inside out. This deeper understanding will enable you to talk authoritatively and excitedly about your company with all whom you meet.

While you're at it, become familiar with your company's promotional materials. This is important for two reasons. First, you want to represent your products and business opportunity truthfully and consistently. Second, you can use these materials to do your "selling" for you. This will leave you more time to build relationships.

Step #3
Assemble your prospect list

Prospects come in all shapes and sizes, ages and backgrounds. No wonder there's no one way to approach them all. What works for you may not work for them. That's why we believe in balancing *warm* and *cold* calls — and adding *retailing* to the mix. Used together, they will strengthen your presentation skills and increase your prospect pool. Let's examine each of them.

Warm calls

Warm calls are just that — calls you make to individuals who may be responsive to your products, services and/or business opportunity. Note the word *may*. Just because you know someone doesn't guarantee anything. All it means is that you're more likely to get an audience.

The Concentric Circles of Prospecting

#3–Cold

#2–Warm

#1–Warmest

You

You compile your list of warm contacts in concentric circles, as illustrated above. The innermost circle, #1, is your warmest "market." It includes prospects you know well, i.e., family, friends, neighbors, co-workers, etc.

The next circle, #2, is not quite as "hot" as #1. Within it you'll find acquaintances from your gym or child's school, for example, or from religious, social and professional organizations. Service providers (e.g., hairdressers, repairpersons, massage therapists) are included here, as are prospects suggested by others (e.g., friends of friends).

The outlying circle, #3, comprises your cold prospects. These include total strangers and the "cool" prospects at the very edges of Circle #2. We'll talk more about cold lists later.

Compiling your "warmest" list will be easier and quicker than you think. Dozens of names will automatically pop into your mind. Thumb through your address book, and you'll find dozens more.

Go beyond the boundaries of your local community, however. Usa, for example, is expanding her business into her Thailand, where she has many warm connections.

Finally, be inclusive, not exclusive. By that, we mean don't make assumptions about who would or wouldn't make a good prospect. Don't assume that someone without a college degree won't recognize a great opportunity, for example, or that someone in her late 60s won't have the drive to grow a solid business. Don't assume that a successful CEO won't be interested in starting from the bottom, or that a mother of five has no time to earn extra income. Remember, network marketing is the great equalizer. Give everyone an equal chance.

For the record

Some network marketers recommend against prospecting family, friends and colleagues. Doing so, they say, creates tension, even resentment.

We think they're right ... sometimes. Relationships can become strained. But they can also deepen. It all depends on interpersonal dynamics. With a bit of foresight and smarts, you can avoid sticky situations, opting instead to present your business opportunity and products to the right people, at the right time and in the right way.

Qualifying and prioritizing your list

Now that we've got you assembling your list, home in on your most promising prospects. Take seven names from your "warmest" and "warm" circles and list them on the Prospect Rating Sheet on page 85. Why? To illustrate the point that not everyone you know or love will be interested in your opportunity or your company's products. Some won't even give you the time of day. Difficult as this may be to accept, it's their prerogative. Don't try to force the issue or lay on the guilt. Move on. You wouldn't want them as distributors anyway.

That said, you can limit the number of nos you get by "qualifying" your list.* In other words, you can gauge a prospect's receptivity by giving each of your prospects an "interest score" on a scale from 1 to 10. A "1" would be the lowest score possible, a "10" the highest. Some examples:

Cousin Bob (from your "warmest" list)

Bob is a terribly negative person who's stuck in a job he hates, but won't leave. He seems to enjoy belittling others, especially if they seem happier and more successful than he. As much as you love him, you know that short of a personality transplant, he'll never change his ways. Bob's score: 1. His score likely will stay the same even a year from now.

Neighbor Carly (from your "warm" list)

Carly is the single mom of three. Upbeat and energetic, she's also terribly busy. She works nine-to-five and is a semester away from completing her bachelor's degree. The thought of starting a successful home-based business has enormous appeal for her — but not at the moment. Carly's present score: 6. In the future, however, her score might well be a 10.

As you can see, rating your prospects can help you anticipate how ready, willing and able they might be. Put your highest-scorers, a.k.a. most serious prospects, at the top of your list. These patient and supportive folks will truly listen to what you have to say. Even if they don't become distributors, they can offer constructive feedback on your presentation, as well as the names of other prospects. They may

---

*We have put the word qualify in quotes purposely here. Usually, when we talk about qualifying a list, it's a list of prospects that has been purchased from a company, service, etc. Several hundred to many thousands of names may be on it, not all of them current. Checking the list's accuracy is difficult and sometimes impossible. Still it's important to make the attempt, given the costs of purchasing names in bulk. We'll discuss this subject in greater detail in Chapter 6. Note too that in Chapter 7, we'll discuss qualifying prospects en masse via the Internet.

Prospect Rating Sheet

Warmest Prospects	Present Rating	Future Rating
Example _Cousin Bob_	1	1
1.		
2.		
3.		
4.		
5.		
Warm Prospects		
Example _Neighbor Carly_	6	10
1.		
2.		
3.		
4.		
5.		

Hear ye! Hear ye!

Want to work your warm list quickly and effectively? Then follow the advice of Kim Klaver, a.k.a. Ms. Stud, network marketing expert and author of *The Truth ... What It* Really *Takes to Make It in Network Marketing* (Max Out Productions, 1998). Send a personalized "Dear Friend" letter to 100-plus warm prospects.

Tell them about your new and exciting business and how you're looking for a few bright, ambitious people wanting to earn extra income or make a career change. Ask if they have suggestions.

Share information about your products and their benefits. Offer to forward samples or promotional materials. Provide contact information and end on a upbeat, no-pressure note.

Will all prospects respond? Only those that are truly hot contacts. Moreover, Klaver notes, you'll have worked through 100 names in one fell swoop without having to make the same number of individual contacts.

also sign on as retail customers.

What should you do with your low scorers? Well, the jury's out on this one. Some of the industry's top earners believe you should never, ever cross a prospect off your list. Network marketing guru Mark Yarnell is one of them. Yarnell, co-author of *Your Best Year in Network Marketing*, puts it this way: "Do not, under any circumstance, attempt to determine in advance who is qualified and who is not, who may be interested and who will not be, who is approachable and who is not." Circumstances change, and so do minds. Someone uninterested in becoming a distributor one day may become interested the following week, month or year. Perhaps he's just retired or been laid off from work; perhaps she wants to switch careers or supplement her family's income. These low scorers can become high scorers overnight. Each would have made a great distributor had you maintained contact.

Further, don't prequalify prospects based on your own

assumptions. Just because someone works a menial job doesn't mean he can't build a multinational organization, or that a successful doctor would find network marketing beneath her. The bottom line: Don't ever close a door. We agree.

But we also agree with other network marketers who advise that you purge from your list all prospects clearly cool to your company, its products or the network marketing model in general. Sure, you should give them the benefit of the doubt by following up a time or two, but if they still don't hear the call, put your energies into finding those who do. In short, go with winners only.

So, where does all this leave you? Somewhere in the middle, and that's just fine. Our experience shows that it's good business practice to close the door on some prospects and keep it open for others. We have no set formula for making these decisions; we just use the sixth sense we've developed over the years. You'll develop this sense too.

Before moving on, we'd like to suggest yet another way to organize your prospects. Most simply, group them into categories. For example, as you look over your list, note the individuals who would be most interested in earning extra income, changing careers, purchasing products, etc. This allows you to approach one group at a time, which has two advantages: 1) You'll develop a repertoire of presentations, polishing each one as you go along; and 2) It becomes that much easier to respond to prospects' questions and concerns, and to follow up with targeted phone calls and materials.

Should you approach only affluent prospects?

Here's yet another example of how network marketers differ in their approaches. This one has to do with a prospect's financial status.

Some believe you should approach anyone and everyone, no matter what their economic status; others say, only approach individuals who have already achieved wealth, however that may be defined. We fall somewhere in between. Here's why:

About half of our best distributors had high-powered, lucrative careers before they joined our organization. Accordingly, they didn't have trouble envisioning financial success. Better still, they were realistic about what it would take to build their businesses. In short, they were serious players. They expected to make hundreds of thousands or millions of dollars.

The other half of our distributors had not enjoyed financial success prior to network marketing. Some had dreams that were like their lifestyles: modest. Others didn't have the skills to advance their careers or command big bucks. Still others weren't looking for careers as much as ways to supplement their incomes. Thanks to network marketing, all wound up achieving far, far more than they had thought possible. Some, in fact, have become top earners.

That's why we believe you shouldn't discriminate or make assumptions about who will or won't be a hot prospect based on financial status. If you did, you wouldn't even think about recruiting people like us — an immigrant with few skills and a not-terribly-successful network marketer. What a lost opportunity that would have been! By the same token, you might not think about prospecting those who have already achieved great wealth. You'd assume they'd be happy, when they might well be seeking a career change or new ways to create greater wealth.

Therefore, we recommend that you look beyond dollar signs to other telltale signs: an upbeat personality, a creative yet practical mind, a hungry look about the eyes and a fire burning in the heart. Prospects with these qualities are nuggets of gold.

Cold Calls

Cold calls. What an awful expression! And what images it conjures up! You imagine your heart stopping cold. You can almost feel yourself shiver inside. You fear your words will freeze in midair, that your prospect will give you a chilly response, an icy stare.

We hate to admit it, but these are legitimate concerns — but that doesn't mean you shouldn't cold call or that only warm calls guarantee results. A warm lead may well be a cold lead if the person you're approaching has zip interest in your business opportunity. Accordingly, it's important to use both approaches.

We certainly do. For example, while we're on line at the post office or exercising in the gym, we make a point of socializing with others. Should they seem open to new ideas, we tell them about how we built a profitable home-based business working part time. Often they want to hear more, and so we tell them. Before we part, we hand them a business card and ask if we can send them an informational packet. We assure them we're not trying to sell them anything; rather, we only want to share an opportunity. As you can see, this kind of cold call can quickly become a warm call. Had we restricted our efforts to making only warm calls, we would have missed important leads.

Cold calling can take other forms; among them:*

- Distributing buttons, bumper stickers, calendars, magnets, note pads, T-shirts, canvas bags.

- Distributing fliers and business cards in well-traveled places.

- Producing promotional audio- and videotapes.

- Placing ads in magazines, newspapers and community freebies.

- Running telemercials via an 800 number.

---

* We'll take a closer look at several of these cold-marketing techniques and at ways to increase their effectiveness in Chapter 6.

Hot spots for making cold calls

- Post office
- Gym
- Library
- Supermarket
- School event
- Church function
- Department store
- Doctor's office
- Cocktail party
- Community meeting
- Volunteer organization
- Block party
- Airport lounge
- Classroom
- Concert
- Restaurant
- Child care center
- Seminar
- Anywhere people abound and there's an opportunity for relaxed conversation

- Purchasing lists of individuals open to new business opportunities and sending letters out via fax, snail mail or e-mail.

- Making presentations at professional associations, church groups, parents' groups, etc.

- Renting facilities for conducting large-scale opportunity meetings.

Are these efforts worth the time and money? Most successful network marketers would say no. Make that a resounding no. They believe you should limit your activities to approaches that have a greater likelihood of success. We tend to agree and yet ... you might get lucky; you might find a golden nugget. As mentioned in Chapter 2, you don't need to recruit a downline of thousands to *have* a downline of thousands. All you need is a handful of committed individuals. You may well find one or two of them through cold calling.

Here's another reason to incorporate cold calling in your repertoire: Cold contacts are limitless, while warm contacts may cool with time. This happens when you exhaust (but only temporarily!) the list of prospects you know well. You then must seek out the personal contacts of your personal contacts. Many of these will be cold calls.

Finally, three pieces of advice for developing your cold-calling skills: Practice, listen and respond. *Practice* conversing with strangers. Strike up conversations at the supermarket, in your doctor's waiting room or on the sidelines of your child's soccer game. *Listen* not just to what people say, but to the meaning behind it. What is it that these individuals most want in life, and how can network marketing in general, and your company in particular, meet their needs? *Respond* with good eye contact and body language, and should it be appropriate, with materials about your product line and ways to launch a home-based business.

Retail sales

Warm calls, cold calls. As discussed, we need to do both if we're to expand our organizations. We also need to retail our products if we're to put ourselves in the big league.

One staunch proponent of building your network marketing business via retail sales is Keith Laggos, publisher of *Money Maker's Monthly*. He gives these reasons, and they're great ones:

- **Retailing creates a loyal customer base and repeat business.** Happy customers spread the word, recruiting others in the process. In essence, they prospect for you. Not a bad deal.

- **Retailing is itself a powerful prospecting tool.** You don't have to convince customers of anything; they're already converts. They know your company is credible and have experienced its growth firsthand. They even know how to sell products to others based on your example. This makes it much easier to take them to the next level, namely, to become distributors. Not everyone aspires to build an empire, after all.

- **Retailing can build your business more quickly**, especially if you're more comfortable selling products than a business opportunity.

■ **_Retailing provides a regular source of income._** Depending on your circumstances, this may well be enough to meet your financial needs. Retail sales do more than that, however. In fact, they can help you build an enormously profitable business. That's because they build your personal group volume, making you eligible for company discounts, bonuses and other incentives.

   The same holds true for your customers. The more they sell, the more they make, and the greater their incentive to increase their volume _or_ become distributors themselves. A major selling point for retailing then is that you need to recruit fewer individuals. According to Laggos, if you get your customers to sell five times the minimum volume, you'll need only one-tenth the number of people in your downline.

■ **_Retailing keeps you on the up and up._** If your focus is on recruiting distributors rather than on selling products, you're doing your company and network marketing a disservice. The industry has fought long and hard for legitimacy. Don't blow it. Quality products and services should — indeed must — be at the heart of all that you do.

   With the above in mind, review your warm list and identify prospects who'd make great customers. Think too of ways cold-calling techniques could be used to expand retail sales.

Step #4
Work your list

   While having a long list of leads is great, it doesn't get you anywhere if you don't work it. After all, a name on a piece of paper is just a bunch of letters, nothing more than a missed opportunity.

   On the day we entered the network marketing business, we

Two a day

Previously, we've mentioned the importance of meeting with at least two prospects daily. We were given this advice from the No. 1 earner in Russ' company, and it has guided us since. In fact, we credit much of our success to that one suggestion.

Two contacts a day equals 730 prospects a year. Out of that number, we have found the nuggets of gold who have helped build our organization. We suggest you too commit to this approach.

Making this commitment is serious business, which is how it should be. Prospecting haphazardly or only when you feel like it doesn't cut it, not if you're determined to achieve lifelong prosperity. If that's not your aim, you're in the wrong business.

We know how difficult, even scary, it can be to identify two individuals, let alone set up meetings with them. We've been there, done that. Nevertheless we know — and we promise — that it gets easier. Remember, success is a muscle that you build over time. With each success you get stronger, and meeting with two people a day becomes less daunting.

Do we really meet with two prospects every day? Sometimes it doesn't work out that way, but not because we haven't tried our hardest. And that, perhaps, is what's most important. For as we learned from Mike Hernacki in his book *The Ultimate Secret to Getting Absolutely Everything You Want* (Berkley Publishing Group, 2001: "In order to accomplish something, you must be willing to do whatever it takes to accomplish it." In other words, when you "form an intention and keep fast to it, you will eventually achieve the results you want." We've stuck fast to meeting with two prospects a day, and the results have been nothing short of phenomenal.

promised ourselves we would approach at least two prospects a day. Some 30,000 distributors later, this practice still holds. Which is not to say it's the right way for you. Lifestyle, responsibilities, schedule — all will influence when and how you prospect. Some network marketers, for example, make their prospecting calls on weekends only. Others go full throttle for a solid week a month. Whatever works for you, works.

Nonetheless, it's important to set goals for yourself. Be ambitious but realistic about the number of contacts you will make. Whatever you do, don't make calls just to say you've made them. Quality, not quantity, counts. Racing through a dozen calls won't increase your chances of recruiting distributors, but it might well ruin them. Prospects know when someone is using them, and they'll turn off immediately. What a waste! The whole point of prospecting is to turn people on.

Goals are important for yet another reason: They help you see beyond the present. As you may or may not know, about 70 percent of distributors give up after the first three weeks. Expecting overnight success, they quickly become frustrated. Rather than continuing to work their lists, they make fewer and fewer contacts, until they all but guarantee their failure. As you can see from the schematic on Page 95, this is a pity, given the progress they might well have made beyond the third week. Please don't fall into the same trap.

If the idea of working your list scares you, have no fear. We'll walk you through specific techniques in the following chapter. For now, however, let's turn to a more immediate issue: managing your list.

Beyond Week 3*

Week #1
Distributors = 1

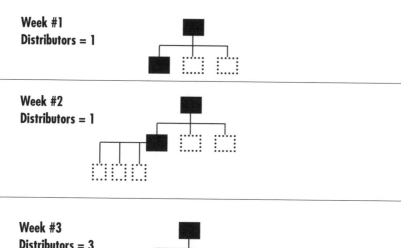

Week #2
Distributors = 1

Week #3
Distributors = 3

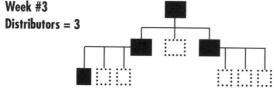

Week #4
Distributors = 6

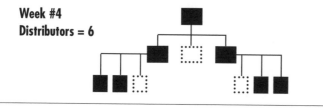

Week #5
Distributors = 14

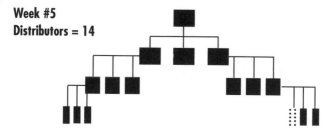

* This schematic is for illustration purposes only and doesn't purport to represent the growth of any one distributor's downline.

Step #5
Manage your list

If working your list is essential, so, too, is managing it. That means gathering key information on your prospects, such as:

- Name and age
- Address
- Work, home and fax numbers
- E-mail and snail mail addresses
- Best times to contact
- Marital status
- Number of children
- Profession
- Professional goals
- Personal goals
- Financial goals
- Community affiliations
- Hobbies and pastimes
- How referred to you

Add to this list whenever or however you can (without invading anyone's privacy!). The more information you gather, the easier it will be to approach prospects and build rapport.

Next up, create a detailed record of any and all prospect contacts. Doing so will jog your memory days, weeks or even months from now. For example:

- "April 3. Met Joe Marlin at his home. Nice guy. Soon to retire from military. Seems very interested in becoming distributor. Suggests I check back in a few months."

- "April 3. Called Ann Yarrow after dropping off sample kit. Likes the product line but doesn't want to become distributor. Interested in becoming a customer. Wait until she tries products for a month or two, then follow up to suggest she become distributor to purchase products wholesale and retail to friends."

- "April 3. Met Barbara Latino at school function. Second child due in summer. Thinking of quitting job, finding something closer to home. Told her about company. Receptive, but preoccupied. Gave her company brochure and Web site address. Will contact again after baby is born."

- "April 3. Follow-up with Steven O'Donnell. He needs to talk the business over with his wife, who's out of country visiting relatives. Will call next Friday."

Having this kind of information at hand lets you pick up with prospects where you left off. It also helps you create a schedule, or tickler system, for making your follow-up calls (e.g., Joe Marlin in

Think follow-ups are a pain?
Think again!

Follow-ups are an inevitable part of the prospecting process, and a welcome one. That's because serious prospects need time to assess their level of commitment, study a company's products and compensation plan, and consult with their significant others. They'll have questions to be answered, concerns to be addressed. And that's where you come in.

By following up and following through, you give serious prospects the information and reassurance they need. Sure, this takes time, but it will be worth it in the end. It's better to recruit a serious distributor over the course of days, weeks or months than to sign up one who jumps *into* the business as quickly as he or she jumps *out*.

June, Ann Yarrow in a couple of months, Barbara Latino in the fall and Steven O'Donnell next week).

You can organize your contact information in any number of ways. Some network marketers use index cards on which they print pertinent information. Others use desk calendars and organizers. Still others use Palm Pilots and/or specialized software to manage their database and/or tickler systems (e.g., Act! My Contact Manager, Sidekick, Filemaker Pro, etc.). Ask fellow network marketers for their suggestions, or experiment to see what works best. Ultimately, the type of system you use is unimportant, that you have one is.

Step #6
Managing you!

Just as managing your list is essential, so too is managing *you*. You're the engine driving your business. Why sputter along when you could be moving at a steady clip? To do this, you need time, space and support.

Time

Excellent books on time management abound, and we won't attempt to summarize them here. Instead, we'd like to talk more generally about time.

For many of us, time is a four-letter word — a real curse. We can't get enough of it, and whatever we manage to hoard slips away in seconds. No wonder we can't build a successful business. We're simply too busy with the demands of everyday life. To which we say, wake up! The whole point of becoming a network marketer is to take control of your life. Who's in charge here anyway?

To be in charge means taking charge of your time. Sure you don't have lots of it, but who does? Even the most successful of network marketers — and we're talking millionaires here — have only 24 hours a day. However, they make efficient use of their time, and so should you.

We believe efficiency boils down to one word: commitment. When you commit to building your business, heart and soul, you'll find the time you need. It's that simple.

Our experience also has taught us that time, to a great degree, is a matter of perception. Believe you have none of it and — voila! — you have none of it. It's like seeing the glass half-empty. Change your perception, and the glass begins to fill. You find a half-hour here and there to make a few prospecting calls or conduct a home meeting. Any one of these activities may result in signing a new distributor or customer. Not a bad use of 30 minutes. Imagine what you can do in an hour!

Beware of time wasters!

- Interruptions like unimportant phone calls from friends and acquaintances, or everyday tasks that may not have to be done every day (cleaning, food shopping, etc.)

- Activities that can be limited or dropped altogether (daily lunches with co-workers, TV viewing, etc.)

- Tasks that can be handled during your nonpeak hours (straightening up your office, paying bills, etc.)

Even a 15-minute stretch of time can move you that much closer to your goals. It's more than enough time to mail out a promotional packet, order stationery, place a newspaper ad or update your contact list. Any one of these efforts may seem insignificant, but again, it's a matter of perception. Little steps = big results. There can be no big results without them.

The bottom line then is this: There is no amount of time, however large or small, that can't be put to good use. Further, if you can't find 15 minutes out of your day to put toward your business, face facts. It won't grow and neither will you. You're unwilling to make a commitment to your own success, so give up your dream of becoming a network marketer. Move on.

Space

As nice as it would be, you don't need a plush office in which to set up shop. You don't need *any* office. All you need is a bit of space to call your own, be it a desk in the basement or a corner of your bedroom (which is where we first launched our business, by the way).

Really, when you think about it, we network marketers are pretty darn lucky. Unlike the stores we see in malls, we don't need a storefront to showcase our products. And with the exception of sample packets, we don't need to keep an inventory on hand. Our company does that for us. Our needs, therefore, are few, making network marketing the ideal home-based business.

Nonetheless, you do need a set space in which to work. It's important for two reasons:

1. Obviously, you need a place for your things: phone, computer, contact information, office supplies, etc. The last thing you want to do is waste time trying to find what could easily be at hand.

2. You need to lay claim to a "psychological space" of your own. Devote a corner or room to your business, and you'll take your business that much more seriously. So will those around you. They'll understand that that is your office and that they shouldn't enter it (or touch your things) without permission.

And while we're on the subject of working space, let us suggest expanding your definition of the term. For example, we do quite a bit of prospecting "on the road." At the gym, the library, even at the doctor's office, we're always talking to people and telling those who seem interested about our business. Our office, in this instance, extends beyond our home or even neighborhood. We take it with us wherever we go.

We each have an additional office in our respective cars. From there, we make cell-phone calls (never while driving!), glancing at our prospect data and goal sheets before we head out to home and hall meetings or to training sessions for our downline. We also have an office in our favorite coffee shop, where we conduct personal strategy sessions as we sip café au lait.

You can have many spaces in which to work.* Why not match them to your mood or the task at hand?

One final note regarding your working space: The less clutter, the more effective your efforts will be. You'll find what you need when you need it, saving precious time and energy.

Support

None of us is an island unto ourselves. We all have ties to the world beyond our businesses. We work full or part time, have families and other social responsibilities. We are part of a community, and with this comes a whole set of duties and responsibilities. We must meet each of them. It's part of being a good and well-rounded person. It's also a good business move, for we need the support of others if we are to achieve success.

If we want support, we must bring others into the loop. We must let them know what we're up to, what we plan to achieve, what we'll need to succeed and how all parties will benefit. The latter point is especially important, as change, even for the better, can make

---

* Should you have absolutely no space in your apartment or home, don't despair. We know many successful network marketers in the same position. What we suggest is that you create a "portable office." All you need is a box or two in which to keep your "tools of the trade." Boxes can be accessed and stored easily, even in the tightest of spaces, and you can take them with you wherever you go (in the car, on vacation, etc.).

others uneasy. Their future is uncertain, and they will need reassurance. Give it frequently. And be reciprocal. If you want loved ones to be cheerleaders, you must do the same for them. Encourage them to pursue their own dreams, and give them the time and space they need to do so. Together, you can become an unstoppable team.

Just as importantly, *be serious*. You can't expect others to respect your time, space or efforts if you don't. At times this may require that you be stubborn or seemingly selfish. It may even make you unpopular with friends and family, or the recipient of harsh criticism. Hang tough. Stand up for your dreams. If you don't, who will?

Finally, should the going get tough, *get going*. Find support elsewhere, from your sponsor, fellow distributors or individuals who may not be in network marketing but who are upbeat thinkers and doers. Meet regularly to share your vision and goals, and to report on your progress. Challenge each other to reach greater heights. Be there when the other needs a boost or simply a willing ear.

Three ways we've used these strategies

1. When the two of us decided to work together, we committed to giving our business everything we had in its initial, critical months. That meant working days, nights and weekends, calling friends of friends, attending meeting after meeting, and reading and talking to all we could to increase our knowledge and skills.

Having set specific goals for ourselves, we needed a way to track our progress. That's when we began using daily and weekly calendars. Ultimately, we came up with what we call the The Commitment Chart, which we recommend you use to jump-start and sustain your network marketing career.

The Commitment Chart

Enter the time spent daily on each activity. Tally your daily and weekly totals.

	S	M	T	W	T	F	S	Weekly Totals
Prospecting								
Home meetings								
Sponsor contact								
Downline contact								
Learning about your company and its products								
Personal development								
Daily totals:								

2. Have you ever climbed aboard a bus only to discover that you didn't have the fare? It's frustrating, especially if you're determined to get to your destination as quickly as possible. We use this analogy because it captures the frustration we experienced during our early days when we'd find a prospect ready to climb on board (or at least meet with us again) and we didn't have promotional materials to give them. Ouch!

We've since become like Boy Scouts — we're always prepared. We don't leave home without an ample supply of business cards, company brochures, tapes and samples. No, we don't walk around like bag people. We keep most of our materials in our cars, so we can replenish our supply as needed as we go about the business of our everyday lives. We never know when a cold contact will turn into a hot prospect. We may be working out at the gym or on line at the supermarket, for example, when we strike up a conversation with someone who has just been downsized. Or we may run into an old friend or neighbor who's seeking new challenges. As the expression goes, you've got to strike while the iron's hot. We, and you, can't do that without getting materials into prospects' hands.

3. Just as it takes money to make money, it takes time to make time. In other words, you've got to take time out of your busy day to make the best use of your day. For us, that means not just looking ahead but also looking back.

For example, every evening we do a quick review of how we spent our time. Our purpose is to identify if, and/or where, we got off track. Did we, for example, meet with two prospects? Did we follow up on leads, talk to our key distributors? Did we get going too late or take too long a lunch break? Did we get to the gym or listen to success tapes? Only by evaluating our results can we use our time to achieve even greater ones.

Chapter 5

Going One-on-one

A s we discussed in Chapter 4, prospecting is central to your network marketing success. You cannot build or sustain a business without it. Hence, the importance of building your warm and cold lists. But lists alone won't get you anywhere if you don't work them. You've got to present your opportunity and products to others — shaky knees and all.

Embarrassed as we may be to admit it, we had shaky knees when we started prospecting too. We were new to network marketing and hadn't a clue as to what to say or do first. Our minds were filled with negative thoughts: *What if no one would listen to us? What if we froze in the middle of a one-on-one or home meeting? What if a prospect belittled our efforts, our products or the industry? What if we failed?*

As you can imagine, we weren't in the greatest mind-set. Luckily, we weren't mired in negativity for long. With persistence, we made headway, and with each new distributor or customer we signed, we learned more about what did and didn't work. We'd like to share that knowledge with you in this chapter. Does that mean we have all the answers? Heavens no, and that's as it should be. You've got your own strengths and style, so put them to good use. How else will you build a business that reflects *you*?

First impressions

As the saying goes, first impressions matter. In our line of work they matter *a lot*. That's why it's so important to present yourself, your opportunity and your products and services in a way that sparks interest and allows prospects to move on to the next level.

Actually, there are three kinds of first impressions. The very *first impression* is made during your initial contact with prospects. Often this contact occurs via telephone. Its purpose is to establish rapport and to quickly and succinctly discuss your reasons for calling. Ideally, this call will lead to further discussion and a meeting.

The *second impression* is made during your first get-together, be it one-on-one or at a home meeting. This is when you make your pitch, using promotional materials, sample products and the like. You'll bring prospects into the fold by sharing the many ways network marketing and your company can help them reach their personal, professional and financial goals.

The *third impression* is also made during your first face-to-face meeting. This one has little to do with the content of your message, but everything to do with you — how you walk, talk, dress, shake hands and make eye contact. That may sound superficial, even trivial, but trust us, it's not. You'll never get to first base, let alone hit a homer, if you turn people off as soon as you enter a room.

Opening moves via the telephone

Even in a high-tech world, there will always be a place for the telephone in network marketing. It may not be as effective as a face-to-face meeting, but it's often the first step toward *getting* that

Your 30-second commercial

In our fast-paced world, you have about 30 seconds to make a good impression, be it in person or by phone. So says marketing and communications expert Debra Koontz Traverso, author of *How to Write a Compelling 30-second Commercial of Yourself* (Blue Island Productions, 2000).

In her booklet, Traverso offers 52 tips for making your first impression a lasting one. Here are but a few, amended for distributors:

- Make a list of what you want to include in your commercial (e.g., your name and company name, the unique products/services you offer, your company's business opportunity, etc.). Weave your company's name into your presentation at least twice. Double exposure means better recall. In addition, use the word "you" as often as possible. This lets others know that you are addressing them individually.

- Practice your commercial aloud and in front of your sponsor and colleagues. Incorporate their suggestions as necessary.

- Prepare a telephone version of your commercial that you can leave should you get voice mail. It should include your name and a message as to who you are and why you're calling. Keep your comments brief, as you never know how much time an answering machine or service will allow. Don't leave your number, however, as people rarely return the calls of those they don't know. Do note that you will call back.

- When making contact, don't try to hasten a relationship or create artificial feelings of goodwill by using first names and informal references. Sounding too familiar and relaxed with strangers will make them uncomfortable.

Three-way calls

When it comes to three-way prospecting calls (you, your sponsor and your prospect), some network marketers swear by them, others swear off them.

Those in the pro camp believe it is a great way to introduce the business to prospects. Having three people on the line makes the call more fun, and gives prospects a better sense of the company's products and compensation plan. Another advantage: Sponsors can use three-ways to train new distributors on the intricacies of prospecting by phone.

Those in the con camp believe such calls are automatic turn-offs. Prospects may feel double-teamed, even resentful. This creates a poor impression.

meeting. Without phones, we wouldn't be able to reach all of the prospects on our list — friends, family and acquaintances, be they across the street or across the globe.

Making calls offers its own set of challenges. At some point you'll be contacting those you don't know well, if at all. You'll have just a few moments to get and keep their attention. Don't assume, however, that these individuals will be less receptive than those with whom you already have a relationship. Sometimes the latter group can be harder to approach.

Whichever the case may be, it's important to develop and then practice some "openers." Although these will be scripted, be flexible. Prospects and their circumstances differ. For example, a busy professional's ears may perk up if you mention a start-up business that has the potential to generate significant income. A working mom may listen more closely if you suggest a way she can work from home and have more time for her children.

When making calls, particularly to individuals outside your circle, consider your timing. For example, don't phone prospects during the dinner hour or much past 9 p.m., when they may be getting kids or even themselves off to bed. Don't call early in the morning, during major holidays (e.g., Christmas) or sporting events (e.g., the Super Bowl). Rather, try calling between 7:30 and 8:30 p.m., or on weekends. Some network marketers suggest you call during the lunch hour, when most folks take a break from their busy days.

When you make contact, identify who you are and how you came by their names. This creates an immediate bond between the two of you. Prospects will think, "If so-and-so sent you, you must be OK." Next up, explain why you're calling. Share your excitement while emphasizing benefits. Here are three sample openers:

1. "Elaine, hi. We have a mutual friend, Kenny, and he was raving about your presentation at the Entrepreneur's Roundtable about today's hottest businesses. There's one more I think you should also know about. I've been in it a year now and it's got incredible potential. If you have a moment, I'd like to tell you about it."

2. "Hi, Mark. I'm a friend of Pauline's. I was telling her last night about a great business I've launched to help me meet my retirement goals. She suggested I call to tell you about it because you're also interested in retiring early and in style."

3. "Hi, Angelica. Your brother Paul insisted I call you because he said you've been thinking about changing jobs so you can spend more time at home with your children. I've got a home-based business opportunity that might be just the ticket. You can make good money from home, working as few or many hours as you'd like."

Ideally, your prospects will want to hear more, but don't tell them everything at the outset. Your goal is to set up an in-person meeting. It's the best way for individuals to get to know you, and to review promotional materials and sample products. Gently nudge them in this direction. Should they be hesitant, suggest that you can send an informational packet with your contact information, and then follow up. And what of those who say no off the bat? If possible, ask why. Often, they'll have concerns you can address on the spot, increasing the likelihood of taking them to the next step.

Making your prospects (and yourself!) feel at home

Home meetings are a great way to present your business opportunity without the hard sell and from the comfort of your home.* As you'll learn, they're wonderfully effective in a number of ways:

- *They bring together several prospects simultaneously,* so you can introduce them to your company's solid history and mission, top-quality products and services and industry-leading compensation plan.

- *They cost little to organize and are easy to schedule and conduct,* allowing you unlimited weekly and monthly opportunities to expand your business at your own pace and on your own terms.

- *They allow you and select others to share actual experiences, or "testimonials,"* so prospects can more fully understand how your success — and that of your downline — can be reproduced.

- *They create a congenial atmosphere,* allowing individuals from all walks of life to share in a common dream and experience the mutual support so typically found among distributors.

---

* By the way, home meetings don't have to take place only in *your* home. Some can be hosted by your sponsor or by one of your distributors. Meetings can also be hosted in the homes of prospects who volunteer to put together a group of interested parties. Should your home be undergoing major repairs or not yet reflect the image you'd like to present, consider these alternatives.

- *They build your confidence and polish your presentation skills,* enabling you to more easily handle questions and objections, more comfortably interact with a wide range of individuals and more steadily expand your business.

Do note, however, that home meetings are not scaled-up cold calls. Bringing "cold" folks into a "warm" home — namely those who haven't been informed of the meeting's "agenda" — is dishonest, and ultimately a waste of time. The only people you want to have walk through your door are those who have a sincere interest in or curiosity about what you have to say. The whole point of home meetings after all is to turn prospects into distributors.

Attendance at home meetings varies, so shoot for 10 guests. This will give you a large enough crowd to warrant the effort, but not too

Put down that fork!

If you're thinking of conducting your first one-on-one meeting in a restaurant, think again.

Full meals take time, something you and your prospects have limited amounts of. By contrast, chatting over a cup of coffee (or tea or soft drink) and light snack, is not only more expedient, but often more effective. Such interactions also tend to be more relaxed, allowing you to spend more time talking rather than chewing. (Seriously, it's hard to get prospects to share information about themselves if they've got food in their mouths.)

Coffee shop get-togethers are not only easier on the waistline, but also easier on the pocketbook. We always pick up the tab when meeting prospects (for coffee or otherwise). They are there at our invitation and shouldn't be expected to pay. You don't want to give them the wrong impression; namely, that you are inconsiderate, cheap or making so little money that you can't afford to pay for a cup of coffee.

many to preclude personal interaction. Now, just because you invite 10 people doesn't mean all will show. Our experience shows that even the most well-intentioned individuals may drop out for any number of reasons. Accordingly, we invite more folks than we think will attend. We also make reminder calls a day or two prior to the meeting, to increase the number of attendees.

Although you may hold some of your meetings during the day, say during the lunch hour, the majority likely will be conducted on weekends or at night. We've found evenings preferable because most people stay close to home Monday through Friday. Saturdays and Sundays also work but can be a bit trickier, as prospects tend to be out and about, running errands, playing tennis, chauffeuring kids to soccer games, and so on.

Evening get-togethers should take place shortly shortly after dinner. This gives prospects time to eat and shift gears after their work days. The timing of weekend meetings is more open. A lot depends on the schedules of your group. For some prospects, early mornings are best, for others, late afternoons. Inquire about preferences as you begin to organize your guest list.

Home meeting logistics

Choose the right meeting space in terms of size and setup, and arrange the seating to create a comfortable atmosphere. Get rid of smoke and pet odors. Clear the room of anything that might offend or distract visitors. Turn off the phone. Make sure the kids are in bed or occupied elsewhere. Don't leave private and/or inappropriate materials lying about. Your visitors may have to use the bathroom or phone in another room, so be sure these areas are clean and orderly.

Hand out name tags as guests enter. Have distributors who are present wear their company pins, especially those that signify levels of achievement. Have all equipment and displays ready and on the

Home vs. hall meetings

If a home meeting is great for recruiting individuals, why not scale it up to a hall meeting that draws scores, if not hundreds, of prospects simultaneously? The answer? Timing and purpose.

Generally speaking, hall meetings are not the front line for recruiting new distributors. That's a two-step process, which usually begins with a promising one-on-one approach, followed by a home meeting.

It is at home that prospects literally make themselves "at home" with the idea of network marketing. The scale of such meetings is purposely small and intimate, so all questions, concerns and fears can be addressed. With that knowledge, prospects become distributors, distributors who then attend hall meetings.

Hall meetings require the participation of several speakers and/or facilitators to provide tips, tools and motivation. Careful planning, coordination and promotion are critical and can be a challenges in and of themselves. There also is the cost. A hall must be rented to accommodate the bigger crowd. You'll also have to provide take-home materials, and, often, light foods and beverages.

There are other cons to hall meetings, according to Mark Yarnell, industry leader and author of *Your Best Year in Network Marketing*. Here are but a few:

- Hall meetings make it easy to fall into the trap of thinking you can build your business en masse, without ever having to prospect one-on-one.

- If poorly attended, hall meetings cast a poor light on you and your business opportunity. (Imagine how much more effective you would have been had you been with those few prospects one-on-one or at a home meeting!)

Continued on Page 114

Home vs. hall meetings (continued from Page 113)

- Hall meetings are public affairs. Some prospects, however, need privacy. Doctors, for example, may not want their patients to see them in a different setting. Teachers may not want to bump into the parents of their students.

- Hall meetings create an "illusion of saturation." When prospects walk into a room of hundreds, all from the same area, they'll mistakenly assume that there will be too much competition and not enough opportunity.

opposite side of the room, away from the door, so late arrivals won't distract you or others.

If you do offer refreshments, make them simple, and offer them after the meeting. Do make drinks available throughout the meeting, however. There's something about socializing with a drink in hand that gets people talking. But steer clear of alcohol, as it will offend some people. Besides, you wouldn't want prospects to limber up too much!

Try to have a greeter available to meet all guests and put them at ease. This person should not only offer a friendly smile but directions on where to sit, get refreshments, find the bathroom, etc. The greeter should seat together individuals who might have something or someone in common, so each can more fully enjoy the get-together.

Should the meeting take place in someone else's home, arrive early so you can familiarize yourself with the setup. Make small talk with your host as you wait for guests to arrive. For example, compliment a painting or discuss an item in that day's newspaper. Discuss a shared interest, be it golf or college-bound children. Be enthusiastic, but sincere.

Start the meeting on time out of respect for those who arrive punctually. Share your agenda at the outset, so your guests know what's to come. Tell them when the meeting will end and stick to your word.

The meeting itself should last 60 to 90 minutes tops, but its end marks the beginning for those who become distributors or are seriously thinking of doing so. Follow-up is critical, therefore. We will discuss how to do that later in this chapter.

A winning presentation

An effective presentation is one that opens the door to new distributors and customers. Note we said, "opens the door." As mentioned numerous times before, not everyone will want to sign on. Their reasons vary and have little, if anything, to do with you. And just because someone leaves your meeting uncommitted or seemingly turned off doesn't mean they aren't interested. You may well have planted a seed that flowers several weeks or months later. All the more reason to prepare a polished and compelling presentation.

When you speak, do so in terms of benefits. Your guests didn't come to hear *your* success story. They want to know how *they* will achieve success, personally, professionally and financially.

Whatever you do, avoid false promises. They reflect badly on you, your company and the industry. Further, they do nothing to build your business. Oh, you may get a few starry-eyed individuals who want to become distributors, but don't be fooled. They won't stay long. Besides, if your company, its products and compensation plan are as great as you say, there's no need for hype.

Although presentations may all have the same components, the components themselves can be presented in any order. Some network marketers, for example, lead with their company's business opportunity, and then discuss products and services. Others lead with products and services, and then move on to compensation plans and the like. Whatever approach you choose, your presentation should include the following:

- Information about how network marketing works and what makes it a revolutionary form of doing business.

- An overview of your company and its unique, high-quality products and services.

- A brief but informative discussion of your company's compensation plan, illustrated in handouts or on a chart large enough for all to see.

- A promotional video and/or distribution of company brochures, starter kits, etc.

- A demonstration of retail products and distribution of samples.

- Testimonials from you, your sponsor and other distributors as to how the business opportunity worked for each of you (e.g., how you've tripled your income, now work part time, spend more time with your family, etc.).*

- A question-and-answer period.

8 presentation pointers

1. Don't get thrown offtrack should only a few of the individuals you invited show up. In our business, it's quality, not quantity, that counts. Among attendees, you may find the invaluable one or two who will help build your organization.

2. Don't feel you have only one shot to sign any or all of your attendees. If they're interested they'll want to learn more, be it at the home meeting or afterward. So take the pressure off yourself. You cannot control what others think or do.

3. Assure prospects that they will not be forced to sign up or buy products. Let them know that you only want to present a business opportunity and introduce them to a great line of products and services. Prepare for objections and address them before they're even raised. This clears the air, so to speak, allowing your prospects to listen more openly to the rest of your presentation. Many of these objections are discussed in Chapter 3. Almost all are fear-based. Prospects, for example, may fear they'll be part of a pyramid scheme or have to plunk down their life savings on products, business cards, ads, etc. Reassure them that just the opposite is true.

4. As nervous as you may be, don't put on airs or act out of character. Prospects want and need to relate to someone just like them. Otherwise, they may think they'll have to become

Dress for success

You're not just presenting a business opportunity at a home meeting — you're presenting yourself. Attendees will look at you to see if you walk the talk and dress the part. Don't worry, you don't have to run out and buy a new wardrobe. Simply keep the following tips in mind:

- Dress comfortably but professionally, and a "notch above" what prospects would likely wear. Be conservative, not flamboyant.

- Dress to the occasion: casual wear in relaxed get-togethers, formal wear in more business-like settings.

- Avoid wearing too much makeup or jewelry, and go light on the perfume or aftershave.

- Don't wear pins or other items that are of a political or inappropriate nature, as that may offend or alienate some of your guests.

something they're not in order to succeed in network marketing. Testimonials are key here, for they put everyone on a level playing field. People love people-stories, and these often are the most informative and memorable.

5. Come up for breath. Don't worry about filling every moment of airtime. Let prospects lend you a hand by giving them an opportunity to ask questions.

6. Don't bog prospects down with every detail about your company and compensation plan, or fill their arms with dozens of brochures, videos and samples. Studies show that most individuals remember only 15 percent of what they've learned the hour before. Accordingly, pick and choose what you say and distribute materials to ensure key information will be retained.

7. Use visuals whenever you can to get and sustain interest. Create charts and handouts that draw on the graphics found on Pages 48, 71 and 95.

8. Give prospects something they can go home with — intangibles such as enthusiasm, promise and the sense of being part of a business revolution. You do this by sharing your excitement and speaking in terms of benefits.

Listen up!

Here's a hot tip whether you're meeting with individuals by phone, one-on-one or at a home meeting: Talk less, listen more. Don't become so enamored with the sound of your voice that you lose sight of your purpose — to share an opportunity and to help others take advantage of it.

To be effective, you must give prospects an opportunity to respond to what you say and to ask questions. No comment or query is trivial. Each deserves respect and a thoughtful response.

Don't interrupt or jump in prematurely, assuming where a conversation will lead. Take the time to follow its course. Listen for objections. Acknowledge what you hear, and then address your prospects' concerns. Your words should be honest and direct but never forceful. You're not engaged in an argument here, just an exchange. The last thing you want to do is make prospects feel intimidated or stupid, or put them on the defensive.

Listen to all parties. When meeting with a married couple, for example, don't speak to one spouse but not the other. At a home meeting, don't focus on just one or two of the individuals present. Divide your attention equally among all.

> **Follow the script!**
>
> If you want to deliver a dynamite presentation, follow the leader, namely your sponsor.
>
> He or she knows the key pointers to present and how best to present them. Accompany him or her to one-on-one and home meetings as an observer. Listen in on prospecting calls (with the permission of all parties, of course). Have your sponsor critique your performance, so you can improve your skills.

Prospects from hell

Do you have concerns about how your guests will respond to your presentation? That's to be expected. You're in a room full of people you may not know well, if at all. Sure, it would be nice if everyone were attentive and open-minded, but chances are you'll come up against occasional party poopers. These individuals are disruptive, argumentative know-it-alls who seem bent on disrupting your meeting and challenging your credibility. And then there are the shy, quiet types who offer no clue as what they're thinking. What's the best way to deal with these individuals? With as much as grace and style as possible. Here are some tips:

Compulsive talkers

Although we want a responsive group, there are limits! Compulsive talkers reach that limit quickly. They disrupt a presentation's flow and make it difficult or even impossible for others to speak up, ask questions or enjoy themselves. You've got to quiet these individuals somehow or risk them taking over your meeting.

Compulsive talkers often want recognition, so give it. Acknowledge their comments and questions with a bit of flattery, saying things like:

- "Mark, that's a great question. Before you go further, let me respond, and then have some other guests comment."

- "Alice, I bet others in this room are thinking the same thing. How about it, folks? Does this hold true for the rest of you?"

- "Noel, you bring up another good point. It's a bit beyond what we're talking about at the moment, but it's important to discuss. How about you and I get together at the break or at the end of our meeting?"

Should you come up against a compulsive talker you can't rein in, take a group break and quietly pull the person aside. Compliment them on their participation, but tactfully ask that they reserve their questions and comments so others may speak. Again, suggest that the two of you get together after the meeting to discuss the important issues that have been raised.

Naysayers

Oh boy, what a challenge (and a pain) these individuals can be. Ideally, you would have weeded out the majority of them prior to your meeting. Still, one or two may slip through.

Naysayers will challenge your every word. They'll find fault with everything you say, and sit with arms crossed and annoyed expressions. How distracting!

But don't let the naysayers do you in. If possible, ignore them. If that doesn't work, try flattery. They, like compulsive talkers, want acknowledgment, so give it, within reason. At the very least, be prepared. Return to Chapter 3, to get the ammunition you need to counter whatever arguments they may raise. (If they're being that negative, they'll likely have more than one.)

Remind naysayers that they came to the meeting voluntarily, looking for something in particular, and that you don't want them to go home empty-handed. Say for example:

- "Esther, I understand why you're skeptical, and that's not a bad thing. We should all be skeptical. I certainly was before I became a distributor for Company XYZ. The last thing I wanted was to get involved in a get-rich-quick scheme. Like you, I don't want hype. I want results. Marty, Shane — wouldn't you say the same holds true for you? Lois? Brad? Agree? But back to you, Esther. You came here tonight for a reason, and I suspect it wasn't to play devil's advocate. So let's put things into a more positive light. Let's talk honestly and realistically about what it would take to launch a successful business."

Should all else fail, have the group take a five-minute break and talk to naysayers privately. Tactfully but directly tell them that their comments are important and that you'd like to respond to each. First, however, you need to take back the floor. Try something like this:

■ "Noel, I need to ask a favor. I promised the others who came here tonight that I would give them the information they needed to become distributors. As part of that, you and I need to give them the floor, so to speak, so they can ask questions. You're very articulate and that may intimidate others a bit. Why don't you hold your comments until later? Then, after the meeting, you and I can discuss whatever else you think is important."

Silent types

Don't panic or make assumptions about what these individuals are thinking. Give them the benefit of the doubt. They may simply feel uncomfortable being in a roomfull of strangers.

Put them at ease through good eye contact and a warm smile. Try to draw them into the conversation by addressing them directly. For example, ask them a question they'd find easy to answer, such as: "Mary, I understand you work one town over. How long is your commute?" (Her answer can then lead into a discussion about the advantages of working at home.) Another approach would be to go around the room and solicit a brief response from all attendees. For example: "What would be the ideal number of hours you'd like to work each week?" or "If you worked fewer hours each work, how would you spend your spare time?"

Finally, make a special point of talking to shy guests during breaks or after the meeting. Let them know you're happy they came and that you're available anytime to answer any questions they may have.

Evaluating your performance

You may be out of school, but grades are still important. Now, however, you must grade yourself. On your presentations, that is.

After a one-on-one or home meeting, ask yourself if you've sparked your prospects' interest. Although there is no exact measure

Performance Evaluation

For the following items, rate yourself on a scale from 1 to 10. Note that there are no failing grades. Your sole purpose is to identify the areas in which you can make improvements:

	Score
Delivery of script	
Response to prospects' questions and concerns	
Body language (firm handshake, good eye contact, friendly smile, proper dress)	
Logistics (setup/adequacy of meeting location)	
Preparedness (name tags, promotional materials, business cards)	
Use of promotional materials (too much/too little)	
Follow up (scheduling of next contact(s)	
Notes	**Total**

for this, you can often get a sense of how well you did.

Think back on your delivery. Are you pleased with how things went? Did you offer a firm handshake and warm smile? Did you maintain good eye contact? Did you speak in terms of benefits and respond to prospects' questions? Was the meeting space adequate? Did you have enough promotional materials on hand? Good visuals? Did you stick to your script and timeframe?

That's a lot of grading! Still, it's necessary if you are to strengthen your presentation skills. Don't worry about perfection. Mistakes are mistakes only if you don't learn from them. Here, as in all other aspects of life, there's a learning curve. Allow yourself to be a student.

To help with your grading, use the rating sheet on Page 123 to help you identify the areas that need improvement. Again, don't be too concerned with your scores. As the saying goes: "If at first you don't succeed, you're running about average." You have to let yourself be average if you are to be great one day.

Follow-up

If possible, set up a time to get back in touch with prospects, be it by phone or in person, one week or one month down the road. Do this before the end of your first one-on-one or home meeting, so you both know what's to happen next. This gives you an important "in" when you do make contact. You can then say something like: "Marsha, hi. This is Bob Casey of XYZ. Thanks again for coming to the get-together (home meeting) at Larry's last week. I'm calling today at your suggestion, to follow up on your interest in becoming a distributor."

Should prospects be too busy to talk or seem uninterested at the time of your follow-up, don't give up. Their response may have little to do with you and everything to do with what's going on in their lives. Perhaps they're in the midst of a work deadline or their children have the chickenpox. Perhaps you simply called at the wrong time — too early or late in the day. Don't assume the worst. Rather, set up another time to talk. Let them know you're available in the meantime, and provide them with your contact information (e.g., phone and fax numbers, snail mail and e-mail addresses).

Call or drop prospects a line thanking them for meeting with you. If you promised to send promotional materials or samples, do so immediately. It's critical that you keep your word. You must strike while the iron is hot. The more time that passes between your initial and subsequent contacts, the greater the likelihood that prospects will forget who you are and what you shared.

Finally — and this should go without saying — it's important to make note of all information garnered through your interchanges. We're talking about more than name, rank and serial number here. Rather, focus on personal data, such as where individuals live and work, what they most want from network marketing (launch a new career, supplement present income, work from home), their marital status and personal interests, etc. These details should be noted *in writing* to jog your memory, for just as prospects may have poor retention over time, so might you. You need key information at your disposal if you are to continue to build a meaningful relationship with prospects. How else can you demonstrate you remember them and care?

Three ways we've used these strategies

1. Prospecting isn't easy, at least not for the novice network marketer. Why should we lie to you? Sure, there are some individuals who love it from the get-go and can do it with enjoyment and ease. For the rest of us, however, it's an acquired taste, a learned trait. Helping distributors become more comfortable and proficient is our single greatest challenge, and we suspect it will be for you too. Here's an analogy you might want to share with them:

Imagine it's a Friday night and you head off to a movie. You've heard somewhere (was it a movie review or a snippet of a conversation?) that the film you're about to see is great, a real blockbuster, and every word turns out to be true. Excitedly, you tell everyone you know about it — family, friends, neighbors, colleagues, even strangers. Some folks are so caught up in your enthusiasm they run out to the theater. Of these, some will share your sentiments and others will go home unimpressed. Other folks won't even go to the theater; their tastes simply differ or they have other things to do.

So here's the question: Would you feel rejected by those who didn't like the film or chose not to go? Of course not! Their response doesn't reflect on you.

Films, network marketing ... if you really think about it, they're one and the same. You share an opportunity, wanting the best for others, who then decide whether or not to take advantage of it. The call is theirs, and ultimately there is little you can do to affect the outcome. So why fear rejection? It's not personal.

We know this is easier said than done. Still it's important — no, essential — that you try. *Reject rejection.* You have other things to

do with your time and energy — namely, to build the business and
life of your dreams.

2. Here's another way to make prospecting more comfortable:
Imagine you are talking not to strangers, but friends. It is easier
than you think. All you need to do is practice.

As Usa mentioned on Page 29, greeting others with a warm,
inviting smile opens all sorts of doors. That's because they smile
back. (Walk away from those who don't.) Their smile will make you
more comfortable, which will make them more comfortable, which
will make you more ... well, you get the picture.

From smiles, it's a lot easier to get into conversations. Here, too,
you may need a bit of practice, as small talk makes many of us
uncomfortable. Where do we begin? What exactly should we say?
Know that there is no one script to follow; that would be akin to
having the same conversation with everyone. Instead, aim to go
with, yet direct, the flow.

According to Beth Mende Conny, author of *The Art of
Schmooze* (Dancing Duck Productions, 2003), it's not difficult to
become a master schmoozer. Each day offers numerous
possibilities. For example, she suggests you make a conscious effort
to talk to people you might normally overlook during the course of
your day — the city bus driver or supermarket cashier, etc. Ask
questions to get them talking about themselves. You'll be surprised
at how much you can learn.

Do the same with those you know only in passing, Conny
continues. Try to remember something about them that you can
bring up in conversation. Examples: "Jill, what a great tan! Did you
finally take that vacation in the Bahamas?" "Paul, how's your
family? Is your son still playing soccer?" "Arlene! I was thinking

about you the other day while reading the newspaper. Your fund-raising drive made the front page. How impressive!" Moral: Pay attention to others and they'll pay more attention to you.

Two other hot tips from Conny: First, never use yes/no questions when trying to strike up a conversation or keep it going. Doing so may shut the very door you're trying to open. For example, instead of saying, "Are you free anytime soon so I can tell you more about my business opportunity?" go with "I'd like to tell you more about my business opportunity. What's a good time to meet?" One allows a hesitant prospect to slip away, the other takes the relationship one step further.

Second tip: When conversations don't go the way you hoped, try not to take it personally; it almost never is. We think that's great advice, which is why we try our hardest to share it with our distributors. Our experience shows that prospects say no for these reasons, among others:

- They're stuck in old ways of thinking, being and believing.

- They're scared of the unknown.

- They aren't willing to make a commitment.

- They aren't interested, period.

- They aren't interested at the present time.

- They're in transition; they have too much going on personally and professionally.

- They're cynical, convinced there's a catch, even when something looks good.

- They don't have enough proof or assurance.

- They don't have enough confidence and/or vision.

- They don't fully understand the network marketing model or product.

3. Along the road to success, we've met many people who have helped us expand our business in large and small ways. We made a point of cultivating them, and you should too. This is especially important when it comes to the key individuals in your upline.

To become a master prospector, develop a strong relationship with your sponsor. She has walked the same road you're on, so why not turn to her for advice and direction? He has experienced your same fears and insecurities, so why not let him share his techniques for moving past them?

Know that your upline includes more than just your sponsor. Your sponsor's sponsor (or even your sponsor's sponsor's sponsor) is someone with helpful tools and tips. Don't be shy about giving him a quick call or dropping her an e-mail. Sure it may be a bit scary to approach someone you don't know well or at all, especially someone you've admired from afar. But don't forget: You're members of the same family. Family come through for one another, for what's good for one member is good for all.

Chapter 6

Beyond the One-on-one

Before diving into this chapter, we'd like to reiterate the importance of building your warm and cold lists, and mastering the art of the one-on-one meeting. We don't know of any successful — or ultrasuccessful — network marketer who skipped either step. They, like we, knew how important each step was to building an empire, and how each gave them an opportunity to learn the business inside out.

That said, meetings and warm and cold lists are not enough. Lists shrink with time; the number of meetings expands. Further, there's only so much of you to go around. Short of cloning yourself, you'll have to find other ways of extending your reach.

You'll find those other ways in this chapter. All of them work, but not for everyone. Much depends on your goals, skills, budget and style. What works initially may not work later on, and vice versa. Nonetheless, we share these ideas to spark your thinking and doing. We also suggest that you try several approaches. As we've learned from experience, you increase your chances of success by working on more than one front.

Become a different kind of sponsor

In addition to sponsoring your distributors, sponsor local activities. Obviously, it's an effective tool for increasing your visibility, but it's also a great way to support your community.* Here are just some ideas for making a difference:

- Sponsor a 5K race to raise funds for breast cancer research.

- Donate products for your library's silent auction.

- Provide T-shirts for your city's Little League team (with your company's name printed on the front).

- Create an awards program for local business leaders.

- Start a college scholarship program for minority students.

- Lead a food drive to benefit homeless families.

- Join the boards of not-for-profits, professional societies or educational institutions.

The time, energy and commitment you put into these efforts will be noted by others, making prospects that much more responsive to your business opportunity.

Thank "repeaters"

Don't focus so narrowly on prospects that you forget the individuals upon which your business is built, namely, your dedicated distributors and customers.

Express your thanks by sending customers thank-you cards for referrals or continued business. Offer discount coupons or free

---

* An interesting point: Studies show that 60 percent of Americans would switch their business to retailers involved in "good works" (provided the retailers' products and pricing were comparable).

products, tying them to special occasions such as birthdays and holidays. Show distributors you care by taking them to dinner on their first anniversary of joining your downline.

Following through on these suggestions is easy, provided your database is up-to-date. Accordingly, get into the habit of jotting down brief notes after each contact. For example, make note of a customer's love of golf or a distributor's vacation plans. Then, should you see an interesting article or notice of a special event, drop them a quick note. They'll appreciate — and remember — your thoughtfulness.

Link to special occasions

Prospecting is a year-round activity and can be especially effective if you link your efforts to holidays, anniversaries and birthdays. For example:

- Offer special discounts or products for moms and grandmothers on Mother's Day, or for dads and grandfathers on Father's Day. Don't overlook other great tie-ins like Administrative Professional's Day, Valentine's Day and Christmas.

- Promote seasonal items, such as gardening products in April or suntan lotions in June.

- Create product baskets targeted at graduating teens or retirees on their 65th birthdays.

Order stationery

For a modest fee, network marketing companies furnish distributors with company letterhead and envelopes. We think it's a great investment. First, they are produced professionally and in color, saving you big bucks on graphic design and printing. Second, your company's logo and tag line are great ways to let prospects know about your services at a glance.

Your stationery package also will include business cards. Don't just hand them out, however. Turn them into miniature billboards by using the reverse side to share additional information about you, your company and your products. For example:

- "I can help you live your dream."

- "Company XYZ — connecting the world through cutting-edge technology."

- "Legal services that put the law on your side."

Another option is to put an inspirational quote on the back of your card, giving people a reason to hang onto it or even carry it around in their wallets. For example:

> *You must have a dream to make a dream come true.*
> —*Beth Mende Conny*

Use testimonials

Ask your top distributors and happy customers to help you spread the word through *their* words. You can then use their testimonials on fliers or in local ads, giving you and your company's products greater credibility.

Go to work

In-home demonstrations are a tried-and-true way of introducing your products and business opportunity. You don't have to stay at home, however. Many distributors are taking their acts on the road and into offices for lunchtime get-togethers.

Ask family, friends and acquaintances if they can organize a meeting. It's a win-win situation: You get to talk to several prospects; they get a break from their busy day to sample products and learn more about a way to escape the nine-to-five work world. (To increase attendance, provide a light lunch or snacks.)

Pool resources

Why go it alone when you and your colleagues can pool resources? Conduct home meetings together or run joint newspaper and magazine ads. Co-sponsor community events (see "Become a different kind of sponsor" on Page 132). Share rental fees for exhibit booths at job fairs and county fairs, or kiosks at malls. Think of other creative ways you can reduce your costs, while increasing your lead base.

Package yourself

Many hospitals distribute "goody baskets" to new moms. In them are gift certificates and product samples from local businesses. Ask the hospital if you can include your items as well, or if you can display your own baskets in the hospital's gift shop.

Give away giveaways

According to guerrilla marketing specialist Jay Conrad Levinson, the average person looks at his or her watch or clock at least 75 times a day. Imagine the subliminal marketing possibilities if they saw your company's name at every glance!

You can order desktop timepieces through trophy shops and mail order outfits. But don't stop at clocks — not when you can also get printed mugs, calendars, plaques, pens, mouse pads and note paper.

Hit the road

Turn your vehicle into a moving advertisement by using bumper stickers, window decals and magnetic signs that can be easily affixed and easily removed from your side doors. You can also print your company's name and tag line on the spare-tire cover of your SUV or RV. And while you're at it, splurge on a personalized license plate that promotes your company, products and/or opportunity.

Wash hands

Surely you've heard the expression "One hand washes the other," meaning you do something for me, I do something for you. Accordingly, give a finder's fee to individuals who refer 10 hot prospects, or do facials at your local health spa (using your products, of course) in exchange for free display space.

Be a ham

As numerous surveys attest, most Americans fear public speaking more than death. Nonetheless, this is one fear that is worth overcoming. Speaking in public is a great way to gain visibility and position yourself as an expert in your field. But don't expect to just stand before a group and hawk your wares. Who wants to listen to a half-hour commercial? Talk about turn-offs!

To turn an audience on, you've got to address issues that concern them. For example:

- How to launch a small business.

- How to spend more quality time with your children.

- How to have a healthier lifestyle.

- How to save costs on telephone services.

Do any of these subjects tie into your company's products or services? Depending on your company, yes. But that's unimportant, at least initially. Your primary goal is to "get your face" out there. This will help you build relationships *and* get the media's attention (see "Use the media," Page 139).

To learn more about public speaking and to perfect the art, join your local Toastmasters International chapter or consult some of the excellent books and tapes on public speaking. In the meantime, practice, practice, practice!

Teach

As noted in Chapter 2, the network marketing model is at last gaining recognition in academia, thanks to the work of Dr. Charles W. King, professor of marketing at the University of Illinois at Chicago, and Dr. James L. Morrison, professor of consumer studies at the University of Delaware.* We hope that in the near future, colleges across America will offer courses on the how-tos of our industry. You can make this information available in the meantime, however, by teaching a continuing education class.

Leaf through any adult learning bulletin and you'll find numerous courses on small businesses, career change, retirement, etc. A class on network marketing would fit right in.

Teaching has numerous benefits. Obviously, you'll have an opportunity to speak to a classroom of hot prospects, but that's just the start. You'll also:

- Help legitimize the industry.

- Develop your public speaking skills.

- Establish yourself as an expert in a particular field.

---

* Drs. King and Morrison have written books on networking marketing. They are, respectively, *The New Professionals: The Rise of Network Marketing as the Next Major Profession*, and *The Mission, The Magic: The Insight on Network Marketing*.

You have a built-in advantage as an instructor: You already have your course curriculum prepared. Simply use this book or any other general network marketing books. Have students follow along, chapter by chapter. (Note: Do *not* use company brochures and product samples. You are there to teach, not to promote. Should program coordinators discover you doing otherwise, you may well be blacklisted.)

Write

It's no coincidence that the majority of network marketing books are written by successful network marketers. They want to share all they know, so individuals like you can achieve similar success. Certainly that was the goal of this book.

We had two other goals, however. First, we wanted a platform from which we could advocate for the industry — the myths that surround our profession must be dispelled! Second, we wanted to extend our influence beyond the network marketing community. A book, we knew, was one of the best vehicles for establishing our expertise and getting media attention. Reporters tend to listen more closely to those who've published books or written articles and booklets. (Consider it their form of prequalifying news stories.)

Writing, we know, is its own art form, and we certainly aren't suggesting that you drop whatever you're doing and dash off to your keyboard.* We are suggesting, however, that you seek out opportunities to share your thoughts, experiences and business-building tools through the written word. You'll find ample

---

* If you do decide to hit the keys, head over to your local library or bookstore first. There you'll discover some great how-to books to help craft and market your writing. You'll also find basic books on grammar and usage, so you can give your words the polish they deserve. If writing still sounds daunting, hire a writer to do it for you. You can find one through writers' organizations, job banks, classified ads, and best of all, word of mouth.

opportunities in your local area. Newspapers, newsletters, magazines and specialized publications — all need articles, even editorials. (Editorials, by the way, are said to outdraw ads 3,000 to 1!) The Internet offers many other venues, as we'll discuss in Chapter 7.

Use the media

You don't have to produce your own television show to get on one. In cities across America, you'll find cable stations dedicated to local news and personality profiles. Many also bring together panelists to discuss key legal, health and technology issues, among other topics. Why not volunteer to participate, so you can position yourself as an expert in your field while subtly promoting your business? (You can do the same with your local radio station.)

You should also start thinking as public relations professionals do. These are the folks who get the news in *news*papers and other media outlets. They provide editors and producers with story ideas (a.k.a. pitches), such as these:

- A service that dramatically reduces monthly phone charges.

- The life story of a once-homeless woman, now a successful network marketer, who earns a six-figure income.

- The launch of a product line that helps reverse the effects of arthritis.

If an idea is deemed newsworthy, the media will likely cover it. Public relations is about convincing them that it is.

Whether you conduct your own publicity campaign or hire a professional to step in, we think it's worth your while to learn more about how the process works. You'll find many good books on the topic in bookstores and libraries.

The right tone

Marketers differ as to the best "tone" for an ad's headline, or hook. Some, like Beatty Carmichael, believe it should be straightforward and gimmick-free; the less said, the better. Example: "A Working Mom's Dream: Earn up to $1,000/wk part time from home!"

Others, like Tom "Big Al" Schreiter, believe it should have a clever twist and specifics to add to its credibility. Example: "33-year-old underpaid bank teller from Weird Falls, VA, shows ordinary people how to save $751 on their tax return by adding just one little form."

Still others, like Kim Klaver (a.k.a. Ms. Stud), suggest ads that read more like those found under "professional positions." Example: "Leaders wanted. National marketing group expanding in XXX area. Looking for someone who has owned or operated a business or has experience in marketing, teaching or public speaking. Fax or send resume to … ."

Advertise

We once heard poetry defined as the best possible usage of the least possible words. The same holds true for ads. You've got to grab someone's attention — fast — and get him or her to act; e.g., to become a distributor, buy your products, visit your Web site and so on. No wonder advertising executives make so much money!

You don't have to be an ad exec to create a compelling ad; however, you do have to follow these principles:

- Identify what you want your ad to accomplish. Is it to recruit customers or distributors? To announce an event or launch of a product line? Once your intentions are clear, choose words that draw "visitors" in and compel them to take action (e.g., to order your products, attend a home meeting, request product samples).

- Think twice before running ads in general publications. They may cost less per lead but garner fewer hot, let alone warm ones. Instead, place ads in publications and sections prospects would gravitate toward. Parenting monthlies, for example, might be a great place to target stay-at-home moms. The "help wanted/business opportunities" section of your daily paper would be a logical place to target downsized workers or those interested in new careers. High-tech weeklies might draw those interested in telecommunications products.

Here's another reason to avoid general publications. Only a small percentage of their ads get read. The percentage in specialized publications is higher because readers can't get the information elsewhere. These materials are also retained longer, often for reference, giving your ad additional opportunities for exposure.

- Try differently worded ads, even in the same publication, to get a better sense of what works and what doesn't. Make sure each ad speaks in terms of benefits.

- Instead of a one-shot deal, run your ad several times. Some network marketers believe frequency increases credibility. And as a bonus, your advertising costs will be reduced.

- Run your ad locally at first, then when you're sure it has drawing power, hit regional and/or national publications. The larger a publication's circulation, the higher its ad rates.

- Your headline or "hook" will account for 80 to 85 percent of your ad's effectiveness (see sidebar on Page 140). Sometimes your hook is strong enough to stand alone. The only other thing you'll need is contact information.

- Study other ads for ideas. Which turn you on or off? What changes can you make to your copy or layout to make it more effective? If your ad doesn't draw your attention, it won't compel others to act either.

Build your own list

Want to save on direct mail costs? Then build your own list. It's not that difficult, provided you have kept your database current. Within it you'll find the names of your warm and cold prospects. Direct mail these individuals first, then evaluate your next move.

One such move would be to identify local community and professional organizations (e.g., business associations, social clubs, support groups, etc.). Most of them send mailings to members. Ask if you can buy their lists on a one-time basis. (You want to be sure you've gotten your money's worth before committing to additional runs.)

Another option is to research regional and national organizations whose members would make strong prospects. You can find information on these groups by consulting *Gale Encyclopedia of Business and Professional Associations,* which is available in most good-sized libraries.

- Don't run an ad that promises the moon. It's dishonest and reflects poorly on our industry. Sure, you may rope in a few unsuspecting souls. But you don't want these individuals to join your downline. You want committed winners — and realistic ones at that.

And while we're talking about being realistic, take heed: Ads are no substitute for face-to-face prospecting. The leads they generate may well be negligible. Nonetheless, we believe they're worth a shot, at least on an experimental basis.

Mail your pitch

Surely you've heard of direct mail, so much of which is considered junk mail. No wonder it gets tossed without opening: so much of it is of little or no interest. That explains why companies that use direct mail get a return rate of 1 to 5 percent. That rate, however, is considered successful, for 1 to 5 percent of thousands, even millions, is no small number.

To increase that percentage, carefully target recipients, using language that compels them to open your envelope. For far-reaching campaigns, you should use direct mail companies. They provide lists of prequalified prospects, and write and send your copy.

Buying lists on a one-time basis or for a set period of time may sound great, but beware. The world's greatest list will get only mediocre results if your copy isn't compelling. Even if the copy is, there's no guarantee that dozens, or even a handful, of leads will result. There are three reasons for this:

1. Real leads go beyond a mere response (i.e., inquiry). According to the Direct Marketing Association (DMA), a lead is only a lead if prospects review your product and/or business opportunity and *then* take action.

2. Scores, if not hundreds, of letters mailed to names on a

Example of a targeted direct mail piece

Dear XXX:

Like you, I'm a working mom, and I know how tight schedules and money can be. That's why I started my own home-based business.

It took time to launch, but it was worth the effort. I now work part time, earning twice what I used to. Best of all, I have time for my kids.

I'm now expanding my business in your area and am looking for moms like me who are determined to improve the quality of their lives and the lives of those they love.

I'd love to share more of my story with you. Let's talk this week.

Here's my number: 800-xxx-xxxx. In the meantime, take a peek at my Web site: www.xxxxxxxxxx.com.

All the best in the meantime!

XXXXXXX

list may be undeliverable. (The return rate can be as high as 20 percent.) People move, often without leaving forwarding addresses, and it's impossible for any company to keep track of them. The result is that a list becomes diluted over time. Not surprisingly, then, the more current a list is, the more it will cost.

3. As appealing as it may be to blanket the universe with your copy, the price tag can be high. In addition to postage and processing, you'll have to buy or rent your list. Generally, you'll be charged either a flat rate or a fee per name, which can range from 10 cents to $10. No wonder some network marketers limit the number of mailings or steer clear of them altogether.

When mailing to a small prospect list, say of 100, consider enclosing promotional materials (e.g., a product sample, coins, etc.). Most people can't resist opening an envelope or box that contains something free. According to Keith Laggos, publisher of *Money Maker's Monthly*, envelopes that have a personal and/or compelling message are opened about 50 percent of the time. Postcards, he says jokingly, yet seriously, are opened 100 percent of the time. They have another advantage: They're less costly to produce and mail. (See Page 145 for more on postcards.)

A few last things regarding direct mail:

■ Don't send your mailing without giving thought to yearly calendars and consumer buying habits. For example, some studies find that certain months of the year are better for promotions. The best is December, followed by November. The worst (in "ineffectiveness" order): February, July and January.

Note: Should you decide to do your own mailing, you can print mailing labels via software bundled in with most word processing programs. You can also buy stamps online through companies like Pitney Bowes. To use this service, you will have to rent or buy the company's equipment. These stamps can be merged right into your mailing program.

The DMA reports that consumers are most attentive to direct mail in September, followed by October, then November.

- Devise a way to track the effectiveness of your ads. In other words, include slightly different contact information in each one. That way you can tell how well an ad worked and where it was placed. Here's an example:

Prospects respond to:
Weight No More
P.O. Box 8888
Anytown, USA (placed in a free monthly)

Prospects respond to:
A Thinner You
P.O. Box 8888
Anytown, USA (placed in your daily newspaper)

Post your success

When conducting a direct mail campaign, don't overlook the postcard. That small piece of paper can pack a wallop — and it costs less to send.

The advertising principles outlined previously apply to postcards as well, with one exception: Both sides of the piece must grab attention, as it may be delivered reverse side up.

Play with a full deck (and coupons and fliers)

Deck cards, like playing cards, come — surprise! — in a deck. Prewrapped, the deck includes two-sided cards promoting specific products, services and companies. Coupon books work similarly. Both are disributed free to consumers.

Deck packs and coupon books are mailed en masse to all households within a community or city, rather than to targeted groups. Ad fees are based on the number of participating advertisers and the size of the print run.*

Like ads, deck cards have drawbacks. According to Laggos, only 10 percent of recipients open them. Those who do, tend to scan the very first and very last cards. To make your card stand out, you'll need to pay extra for placement. But even that might not be enough. Cards get tossed because they're of little educational or informational value. They are retained only if they offer some kind of loss leader or free offer, which increases the unit cost of your mailing. It may, however, be worth the additional expense if it opens the door to a second contact.

On to fliers. They can be targeted two ways: first, by wording that appeals to specific populations (e.g., mothers, athletes, downsized workers, etc); second, by their placement (e.g., in child care centers, at health clubs and job fairs, etc.).

Fliers are less expensive to produce and more versatile than deck cards and coupon books. That doesn't mean they should be slapped together, however. If they look unattractive, so will your business opportunity.

Now that we know the differences among these methods, the question is, do they work? Yes and no. Consider this: Your response rate for deck cards and coupon books will be less than 5 percent, maybe even as low as 1 to 2 percent.** So why bother? A good question, but they might be worth the risk if they draw two or three, or even one, new distributor. For as we said in Chapter 3, you don't need to recruit thousands to build a solid business.

---

* Deck cards and coupon book companies have personnel on hand to write copy and/or design ads. There are additional fees for these services. To find companies that specialize in these products, look under "advertisers" in your Yellow Pages.

** These figures are for all sales, not just those in network marketing.

Dial up, dial in

Let your fingers do the walking as you do the talking. We're not talking about one-on-one or three-way calls, as discussed in Chapter 5. Rather, we're talking about new and effective ways you can use your phone to prospect locally, nationally or even internationally.

According to Jay Conrad Levinson, these methods can generate big bucks. Some $370 billion in annual sales are generated from the 100 million sales calls made weekly. Here then are some great ways to make the most of your telephone.

Get an 800 number

They're less expensive than you think. Offered by most local phone companies, they allow your 800 calls to be redirected to your office or home line. You pay a set monthly fee ($0 to $5), plus a per-minute charge, which may range from 8 to 15 cents per

Telephone tips

- Practice your presentations or interactions with friends.

- Minimize background noise and interruptions.

- Try to avoid cell phones when possible; the reception can be poor and the calls themselves may be cut off.

- Don't talk too quickly or try to cram everything in.

- Get comfortable with silence; some people need time to think and respond.

- To create greater intimacy, sprinkle your prospect's name throughout the call.

- Keep a glass of water by your phone should your throat get dry or you feel a tickle in your throat.

- Have pens and note pads on hand to jot down key contact information.

- Make several prospecting calls at a sitting to maintain momentum and toughen your skin.

minute for each incoming call. We consider this an effective
marketing tool, as people are seven times more likely to call an 800
number, as the call is free. Another benefit is that 800 numbers add
to your legitimacy. Well-established companies offer this service;
put yourself in their league.

Teleconference

Why stop at three-way calling when you can teleconference with
dozens, if not hundreds, of prospects? You can do this by way of
conference calling and bridge line services, which allow as many as
500 callers to participate. What's the difference between these
services? Traditional conference calls require an operator to
connect all callers; bridge lines allow callers to dial in directly.

Many of today's top network marketers are using both services
to introduce prospects to the network marketing model, as well as
to their products, services and business opportunity. They're also
using them to support their downlines, conduct seminars or bring
in guest speakers (e.g., industry leaders and motivational
speakers).

To better understand how these calls work, experience them
yourself. Once you appreciate the wonders of teleconferencing, try
hosting a call of your own. Start with a small group of participants,
then ramp up.

Get a second line and a cell phone

If you're offering a business opportunity, be businesslike. Invest
in a second phone line that you — and only you — use and answer.
This ensures that your 6-year-old won't answer the phone (what a
professional receptionist!) or that you won't miss important calls
because your teen-ager is surfing the Internet. Here are two other
advantages of having your own line: The cost is tax deductible and
you can take advantage of all the great business-building services

your local phone company offers.

The same holds true for cell phones. Just about everyone has one these days. In fact, many consumers are giving up their land lines in favor of cell phones, which offer unlimited calling and services such as text messaging and Internet access.

Cell phones keep you, your prospects, customers and distributors in immediate contact, no matter where you happen to be. Because of that, they are fast becoming a standard way to do business.

Use your menu

Many phone companies offer menu options similar to those you get when calling a credit card company. (Press 1 for this, 2 for that, 3 for the operator, etc.). By offering the same, prospects can listen to your 30-second commercial (described on Page 107); get information about network marketing and/or your company; instructions for leaving a message, forwarding their call, receiving a fax-on-demand or free booklet/sample; etc. You can also have an option for prospects who speak only Spanish, Japanese, French, Italian and so forth.

Although menu options are a great way to get your message out, don't overdo it. Limit the number of caller options to no more than four, and always let prospects know how to return to the main menu.

Send a fax

Use your database to send faxes to prospects and/or distributors. You can send an "ad," incorporating the advertising principles discussed above or announcing new products, upcoming meetings, etc. (Many fax machines, by the way, are capable of sending out broadcast faxes. See your instruction booklet.) You can also contract with companies that specialize in broadcast faxing. Like direct mail companies, they have prospect lists and charge by the number of parties contacted.

An important note: You are required by law to have a header or footer on your fax that identifies your name, phone number, and the date and time of your call. States may also have restrictions regarding unsolicited faxes. Check with your state attorney general's office for guidelines.

Get equipped

No discussion of telephones would be complete without suggestions regarding equipment and services. Here are ours:

- Take full advantage of the services your company offers. As mentioned above, these services can be great prospecting tools, be they call waiting or forwarding, recorded busy or out-of-office messages, unlimited recording time for messages, three-way dialing, caller I.D., etc. (Ditto for cell phone services, which may include text messaging and Internet access.) And while you're at it, investigate your long-distance calling options. It's a dog-eat-dog world in the telecommunications industry, with great deals to be had.

- Choose the right phone. Certain features are must-haves: volume and ring controls, auto redial, speaker, and hold and mute buttons. You also might want to choose phones that have an indicator light for missed calls, a window featuring date and time, and caller I.D.

  We tend to use desk rather than cordless phones, as the reception is better. Think twice before getting a phone with two lines. Chatting on one line while another is ringing loudly in your ear can be distracting, not to mention rude to the other party.

- Get a headset to free your hands and shield you from neck pain. Although you can buy one at stores like Staples or Office Depot, we suggest you splurge on a more expensive model. Some headsets are cordless, allowing you to move about your office or home. (Companies like Plantronics and V-Tech offer headsets; expect to pay $100-plus.)

Moving on

Whew! We've covered a lot of ground and have, we hope, given you some solid ideas for prospecting on a larger scale. Now it's time to extend our reach to millions of prospects around the world via that ofttimes overwhelming medium called the Internet.

Three ways we've used these strategies

1. We believe in covering as many bases as possible. That's why, after all these years, we still use many of the prospecting strategies presented in this chapter. Together they form a coordinated, multidimensional prospecting campaign. Again, that doesn't mean any one method works for us all the time or that we work any one of them regularly. Nor does it mean we haven't outgrown some strategies as our business has grown. (We note our current strategies in #2 below.).

As we tell new network marketers, don't reject any technique outright, at least not without researching its effectiveness or talking with colleagues to learn of their results. And don't assume you have to use any one technique "as is." Rather, tailor each to your needs so you can see what works. Chart new ground; learn from your experiences. We did, though not necessarily the easy way.

For example, when we were starting out we sometimes bought into the promise of a particular strategy, only to be disappointed and none the richer. We've since become very discriminating. We suggest you do the same.

By this we mean two things. First, that you be sensitive to the claims of those (i.e., unscrupulous network marketers) who paint an unrealistic picture of what it takes to build a business. "If you only do XYZ, (take out an ad, walk up to strangers in the mall, do a direct mail campaign), you'll sign customers and distributors by the dozens and be rolling in the bucks." We didn't quite believe the hype; nonetheless, we hoped that the results would be decent at least. We learned quickly, however, that there's no one thing you can do to draw the masses, at least not overnight. (Even multibillion-dollar corporations like AOL can't do that.) Nor will any one strategy work the first time out. (Why do you think AOL disks pop up everywhere?) Repetition is key, as is persistence.

Second, be wary of vendors who guarantee results. For example, some direct mail companies tout their lists of thousands or millions. As promising as these may sound, blanket mailings are not only expensive, but also a waste of time if the individuals on the list have little interest in your products or opportunity. What you need are *qualified* lists, as we explain on Pages 174–178. Even then, be skeptical and test the list on a small number of prospects to gauge the response rate. We do this by rote.

The same caveat can be.applied to publications that claim circulation of tens of thousands. That's great *if* their readers are prime candidates. If not, you've just wasted your money *and* your time.

To protect yourself, do as we did: Ask questions and test your results. In addition, talk to people in your up- and downlines. What have they heard about a particular company?

2. What prospecting strategies work particularly well for us? They vary, depending on where we are, with whom, and what we're trying to accomplish. Increasingly, we are employing those that extend our reach nationally and internationally. Not surprisingly, the Internet is an essential tool, though its value is more indirect than direct (as discussed in Chapter 7). We still use ads, though sparingly, and only in targeted publications. We do few mailings these days, give out lots of samples, teach occasional network marketing classes at area colleges and conduct in-person seminars and conference calls for the general public and our downlines. We do some three-way calls and team-led home meetings to cut the learning curve of our more serious distributors. We place articles in online and printed business publications, and have written two books in addition to this one, to further the industry's growth and that of our downlines. We use just about every special feature our phone company offers and practically sleep with our cell phones. (Where would we be without them?)

As effective as these strategies may be, there are two others of equal, perhaps greater, importance. First, we piggyback on the success of others. As mentioned in Chapter 1, we are students of success, always on the lookout for life's winners and information about how they got to the top of their professions. We read about them, interview them and watch them in action. Much of what we have learned has come through them. In short, whenever possible, we follow the leaders. Doing so gives new meaning to the term duplication.

Second, we take advantage of *everything* our companies offer — Web sites, promotional campaigns and packets, you name it. Why go it alone when we can pool resources, so to speak?

Here, then, is yet another reason why your choice of company is critical. Today's cutting-edge companies are pioneers, tapping new markets and using exciting new strategies to reach them. For example, some companies are sponsoring major motion pictures and strategically placing their products in the foregrounds or backgrounds. Others are renting billboards, running full-page ads in mass market publications, helping distributors set up mall kiosks, etc. Still others have created their own cable networks, airing segments introducing their companies, products and compensation plans that prospects view from home at specified times. What a time-saver for you! Similar systems run via Web sites, where prospects can watch videos or listen to audio clips. Many company phone systems offer the latter via the phone.

The list of offerings will continue to grow, creating tremendous prospecting opportunities for you and your downline.

3. We would be remiss if we ended this chapter without discussing one of your most powerful networking tools: networking. Too few network marketers make use it. Perhaps they're shy ("Oh, I can't talk to strangers!) or lazy ("Hey, why's the word 'work' in network marketing?"). Perhaps they think it will require them to be someone they're not ("I'm not a born schmoozer.") or that they'll have to do something they dislike ("I hate glad-handing."). We think they're wrong. Why else would the word "network" be in network marketing?

There are numerous "hot spots" in which to network one-on-one. For example, many Chambers of Commerce and professional groups and associations hold monthly get-togethers so individuals can meet, exchange business cards and leads, etc. You might also want to join or form a group whose sole purpose is to generate business for its members. These groups might have as few as six members, each of whom is from a different profession (sales, accounting, real estate, health care, etc.). Group members commit to swapping leads by passing one another's business cards to at least two other contacts per week.

Please note that networking is *not* about making contacts so you can use people to serve your purposes. Networking is about creating a mutually beneficial relationship in which each party helps the other *when and if possible*. Results are not guaranteed. That's because the relationship is based on the "you" rather than on the "me." Help others achieve their goals, and they'll *want* to help you achieve yours. For example:

Say you work for a company that offers long distance services. At a friends-of-the-library meeting, you begin talking with a woman who just happens to be an optometrist. You make a mental note of this, not because you want to recruit her, but because you might know some people who could use her services. Over the course of the next few months, you send several people her way. She's grateful for the referrals and makes mental notes as well. Perhaps she'll run across patients looking for long distance service; she might be looking for it herself. Yours will be the name that pops into her mind.

Here, neither you nor she initiated the relationship as a means to generate business. You were merely two people who connected and then extended that connection to others. That is the beauty of networking. It's a natural, feel-good kind of prospecting: a win-win all the way around.

One last but key point: To the greatest extent possible, network strategically with movers and shakers. This suggestion forms the basis of Dr. Thomas J. Stanley's book *Networking with the Affluent* (McGraw-Hill Trader, 1997).

Stanley, the co-author of the bestseller *The Millionaire Next Door: The Surprising Secrets of America's Wealthy* (Pocket Books, 1998), defines networking as a means of "influencing the people who influence the patronage behavior of dozens, hundreds, even thousands of affluent prospects." These are the very prospects we all aim to recruit. In fact, many of our industry's top earners devote their efforts to reaching this group exclusively.

According to Stanley, the best networkers succeed because they offer more than conventional products and services — they offer themselves by serving others in extraordinary and *memorable* ways.

Stanley's book is full of detailed illustrations of how this process works. For our purposes, however, we'll summarize what he identifies as the 12 rules of networking.

First, you identify individuals who belong to the "influence network" from which you want to recruit. *Second*, align yourself with those within the network who will help you gain entry to it. *Third*, do all you can to help others in the group succeed in ways they consider important. *Fourth*, be patient. Instead of expecting immediate payoffs, concentrate on long-term results. Payback, so to speak, takes time.

Fifth, spend more time with opinion leaders of the influence network than you would with your colleagues and peers. *Sixth*, "[s]olicit and obtain business for members of your influence network," rather than for yourself. In other words, become a facilitator by helping networkers connect with each other.

Seventh, raise your profile by sending network members clippings, notes and other materials that relate to their interests; sing their praises to other network members.

Eighth, interact, entertain and engage. Take advantage of social situations that draw network members together. For example, ask them to play golf, go to a concert or join you for dinner. *Ninth*, join other influential networks and serve as a bridge between them. *Tenth*, to maintain your credibility, recommend to network members only those individuals and/or companies that provide knock-out service.

Eleventh, "donate your intelligence." For example, volunteer to lead seminars that spotlight your expertise or lend your skills to fund-raising drives for causes your influence network embraces. *Twelfth*, recruit new members to the network, allowing you even greater opportunities to make use of Rules 1–11.

We think Stanley's ideas and book are brilliant, but what if you don't have access to the affluent networks he writes about? Are you out of luck? Heavens, no! We certainly weren't members of such groups when we started out. We knew, however, that our "position"was to a great extent a reflection of our beliefs. If we believed we were below others, that's where we'd remain. That's why we began purging all self-limiting thoughts from our minds (as we discuss in Chapter 8). That's also why we purposely prospected those above us economically. Each of these new customers and distributors raised us yet another level, expanding our influence network.

Accordingly, we suggest you take stock of your current network. Stanley's rules can be applied to it as well. Prove your value, expand your influence and you will join and help form more powerful networks.

Part 4

Prospecting on the cutting edge

Chapter 7

World Wide Web, Worldwide Reach

Be skeptical of anyone who says you can make money on the Internet. Be skeptical as well of anyone who says you can't. If it seems we're being contradictory, we're not; both statements are true, as we'll explain. Let's begin with the first.

A scant 11 years ago, the World Wide Web made its debut and thousands of start-up businesses jumped on the Internet bandwagon. Venture capitalists with stars and dollar signs in their eyes quickly followed, and before you knew it, thousands of Web sites were being launched. In many ways, the Web was like network marketing — a great equalizer. It didn't matter who you were or where you lived. Age, economic status, educational level — none of that mattered. Your idea, product or service was king.

Fast-forward to the present, however, and you see a different picture. Sure, thousands of Internet-based businesses are still making their debuts, but thousands more are calling it quits. Why? Well, to use a cliché, the blush is off the rose. As many companies have learned the hard way, it takes money to make money, even over the Internet. Just ask the executives at

Look elsewhere for a replacement

You make too much of the Net when you assume that it will completely replace traditional ways of doing business. No new medium has ever done that. Television didn't replace radio. Radio didn't replace magazines. And magazines didn't replace newspapers.

—Al Ries and Laura Ries, authors, *The 11 Immutable Laws of Internet Branding* (Harper Business, 2000)

Amazon.com, a company that has become a household name but has yet, of this writing, to make a profit. Amazon has had to pour millions into site development, as well as into systems for buying, storing, selling and shipping books (not to mention the dozens of other products it now offers). Add to the mix salaries, advertising costs and a host of other traditional business expenses, and you can see why the company faces financial challenges.

Amazon is not alone, however. From what we've read and know firsthand, few Internet-based companies are in the black. The fact that some are means little, however. According to Leslie Walker, *The Washington Post* technology correspondent, even the most profitable dot-coms "are still as shaky as Great Grandma on ice skates."

Adding to the shakiness is competition, and we're not just talking about one company's pricing being better than another's. Rather, we're talking about the sheer volume of sites already on the Web and the thousands more — some 50,000, in fact — joining them weekly. No wonder companies are finding it increasingly difficult to attract visitors, and visitors are having a hard time finding them. If you doubt this is true, go to your favorite search engine and type in, say, "contact lenses." We found thousands of listings at the time of this printing; imagine how many more have been added since. Who has the time or inclination to sort through them all? We certainly don't.

Our advice then is to let go of the "if-you-build-it-they-will-come" idea. It's too risky and expensive. Further, it will lull you into thinking there's little else you need to do to build a business. Nothing could be further from the truth, which leads to our second statement about being skeptical should anyone tell you, you can't make money on the Internet. You can … *if* you shift your thinking a bit and see the Web as a *means,* not an *end.*

As a means, it is an essential component of what Al and Laura Ries call your "Outer-Net" prospecting campaign, namely the various prospecting strategies discussed in Chapters 3 through 5. Outer-Net, Inter-Net — they work in tandem and ultimately lead back to one-on-one prospecting, for it matters little if you can reach millions but can't recruit a few.

Do note that we are not belittling the Web in any way. It's a powerhouse when it comes to increasing your exposure and reaching 94 percent of the world's population, namely, those who live outside the United States. Better yet, prospects worldwide have a way to reach you 24 hours a day, 7 days a week, 365 days a year. Even the most successful of network marketers can't put in those kind of hours! In that sense then, the Internet can be a money-maker. It allows you to extend your reach and thereby fast track your success.

The importance of a Web site

Everyone and their grandmother has a Web site, and we think you should too — *if* your site doesn't replicate that of your company. Consider this: All major network marketing companies have Web sites. They've paid big bucks to develop them, as they should. That's because Web sites are a necessity. All businesses today (let alone public and private institutions) are expected to have one. Those that do not are perceived as being behind the times. Worse, they lose out to the competition.

A comprehensive Web site makes a great first impression. Prospects have instant access to information about product lines, commission structures, customer and distributor support and other benefits. They can also learn about your company's officers, history and projected sales. Add video- and audioclips to the mix, and you have a site that does a whole lot of legwork for you at no cost.

But that's not all. Forward-thinking companies allow customers and distributors to order products and prospecting kits online. Many also offer distributors their own personalized Web pages. If your company provides this service, take full advantage of it. It's certainly less expensive than creating your own site, and can only complement your other marketing efforts.* Nonetheless, we believe you should at least consider launching a site of your own. Here are five reasons why:

1. It's a more personal introduction to your company.

Chances are, many of your prospects will be warm leads. You've met them in person, or through referrals and direct mailings (e-mail and snail mail alike). Others will be "cold leads," who happened upon one of your classifieds or fliers, or through a Web search of, say, "home-based businesses." Both types of prospects want to know more about your company, but they want this information filtered through an actual person — a successful distributor who can give them a closeup view of network marketing and what your company offers. Think of it this way: Your Web site is an online version of a home meeting. You greet your guests at the door (your home page), make your presentation

---

* If your company doesn't have an attractive site with online fulfillment capabilities, you might want to rethink your affiliation. Web sites have become an indispensable marketing tool, which is why we include Internet performance in our list of criteria for choosing a network marketing company. (See the sidebar on Pages 63–65.)

and then answer their questions (via the links and content presented on your other pages).

2. It's a relationship-builder.

Your site does more than relay information. It presents a snapshot of who you are. That's why the sites of so many successful network marketers are highly personal.

"You might find a picture of them standing in front of their house with their dog, or on a recent family vacation, or driving the new car they recently earned from their company," Art Jonak noted in a July 2001 article for *Upline* magazine. "There might be a little write-up about them, their hobbies and interests, why they decided to start a part-time Network Marketing business on the side, and what happened as a result. There's probably a link that says, 'Let me tell you how I've helped other people build nice part-time incomes,' followed by testimonials." Each of these elements facilitates relationship-building.

3. It's a showcase for your expertise.

If you want prospects to join your organization, you have to present yourself as an expert. Your site can do just that by offering tips and tools on building a list, warming up to cold calls, growing your downline, etc. You can even gear your content to specific audiences (e.g., working mothers, retirees, professionals seeking new careers, etc).

4. It's a vehicle for spreading the news.

Thanks to your site, prospects can learn where and when company meetings are held. They can also keep abreast of new product lines, changes to your company's compensation plan, the industry's growth and consumer trends.

5. **It's educational, even fun.**

When we launched our first site about four years ago, it was little more than a few pages slapped together. Our site has evolved over time, and so has our knowledge of the Internet. This time next year (or should we say next month?), we will have learned yet more. That's more than OK. It signifies our growth, and with growth comes enjoyment.

Hot tips for building a great site

- **Familiarize yourself with your company's Web site.** You want to ensure yours toes the company line, so to speak, and that it doesn't duplicate what's already available. You'll also want to identify the pages to which your personal site will link (e.g., your company's home page, product page, compensation page, etc.). These links will give your site depth.

- **Visit other sites.** Identify what you like and don't like about other network marketers' sites. Which are attractive or easy to navigate? Which make a poor first impression or take forever to download? Don't stop at these sites, however. Also visit those your prospects would gravitate toward, e.g., those having to do with home-based business opportunities or working after retirement. What do they offer that you might want to incorporate (in concept only, otherwise you'd be in violation of copyright law)?

- **Recruit a strong team.** If you want to build a great site, let someone else do it for you. You're a network marketer, not a Web master or graphic designer, so put your energies elsewhere.

Web masters and graphic designers are not necessarily one and the same. The latter designs the visuals, while the former programs the site itself. Sometimes you can find the two wrapped in one, or one company that employs both. To find these professionals, ask around. Contact local firms and professional societies for leads. Use search engines to identify likely candidates, most of whom will have online portfolios. Note sites you like and contact their hosts for referrals. Interview two to three candidates, as their fees and expertise may vary widely.

- **Start modestly, simply and slowly.** Resist the urge to incorporate every bell and whistle known to man, at least initially. Complex graphics, audioclips, video streaming, Flash — all can be expensive to create and greatly increase download times.* They may also be unnecessary. Chances are your company already has an absolutely gorgeous, highly sophisticated site, so why not link to it? You'll reduce your start-up costs, yet have access to the "complete package."

  Three other things to keep in mind regarding bells and whistles: First, many individuals set their browsers to view text only. They want to reduce download times and prevent computer crashes. Second, older computers may not be able to take advantage of these features, and their owners may balk at installing new software. Third, not all bells and whistles work cross-platform, meaning they may not work on Macs as well as they do on PCs. Granted, Mac users make up only 5 to 7 percent of all computer users, but we think it's a mistake to exclude them. We're talking several million people here. Within their ranks may well be the one or two distributors who can build your organization.

---

* Even 10 seconds can be too long for visitors to wait. Some studies report that most individuals take just three to 10 seconds to decide whether to remain at a site. Imagine how many of them you might lose should downloads take 30 to 60 seconds or more.

Having said all that, please note that we're not recommending you ban special features from your site; they're absolutely astounding and can make a site more inviting. We're merely suggesting that you be judicious in their use and that they be available to all.*

- **Get personal.** As Art Jonak noted, your site should establish a relationship with your prospects. To do so, consider including any or all of the following: a formal portrait; your life story (how you came to network marketing and what it took to grow your business); snapshots of you, your family and your distributors in various settings; testimonials; etc.

- **Choose a strong, easy-to-remember Web address.** Have no fear; it doesn't have to be a perfect one, for address alone won't drive traffic to your site. There are simply too many sites clamoring for attention, making your Outer-Net and Inter-Net marketing efforts that much more important.

  How do you choose an address? To begin, we propose you think twice about using the name of your company or its products. For example, when we keyed Usa's company's name into the search engine Google, it spit out 31,200 links. How overwhelming to prospects — and how unlikely anyone would be to find her. But that doesn't mean you're out of luck. If you're among the first generation of distributors, for example, a good number of derivative names may still be available. You can still direct prospects to your page within your company's site (XYZ@XYZ company.com/John) or by using an address such as "John-XYZ company.com.

---

* A colleague of ours has an absolutely gorgeous site that addresses many of the issues we've discussed. For example, visitors can opt to skip his opening video with a click of the mouse. He's also created a "system requirements" button that includes contact information for technical support.

A few other suggestions regarding address: Keep it short. Long names are harder to remember, let alone key in. Don't mix letters and numbers, as you would with passwords; they're also difficult to remember. Should you be known by two names, you can always use both. That doesn't mean you have to create two sites,

Search engines — key pointers

- Although there are hundreds of search engines, most individuals use just a few, the most popular being Google. Other favorites include Yahoo! and AltaVista. Remember that the next time you get an e-mail from an outfit offering to register you with hundreds of other engines for hundreds of dollars. The results are questionable.

   Even so, some lesser-known engines may be worth considering. Say, for example, that you want to prospect individuals in Central America. A Spanish search engine may be just the ticket (provided at least one of your Web pages is in Spanish — otherwise your site would be unsearchable). To assess its value and that of lesser known engines, conduct a search and compare the results with those you get from Google and the like.

- Search engines differ in the ways they search. Some rely on metatags, or key words, others on brief descriptions, still others on the number of hits a site receives. Work with your Web master to make your site as searchable as possible.

- Go to search engines periodically and enter your name. Where do you rank? You'd be surprised how quickly this can change. The greater your number of hits and links, the higher your position. Visit sites with higher rankings. What do they offer that you don't? What suggestions might your Web master have for improving your standing?

however. For a modest fee, you can reserve both names, create one site and have your Web host redirect, or forward, all traffic. Say, for example, you are known as Katherine Smith and Kit Smith, and decide to launch your site using the former name. Nonetheless, those who type in KitSmith.com can get to KatherineSmith.com via a redirect.

- **Make it easy for prospects to contact you.** Provide contact information on all pages, including your e-mail and business addresses, and telephone and fax numbers. You might also want to indicate your time zone (for callers in other states or countries) and the best hours to reach you.

- **Make your site interesting and relevant.** That might sound like a no-brainer, but it amazes us how many sites are little more than commercials. Your site must put prospects front and center and give them a reason to return. This is especially important, as some 85 percent of visitors to a site opt not to.

  Accordingly, we suggest you add new content to your Web pages regularly. This might include how-to articles, success stories, updates on your company and its products, a calendar of events, online newsletters, etc. You might also want to conduct contests and surveys, and offer giveaways.

- **Publish.** When you post articles, columns and nuggets of information at your site and then make them available to other sites, you gain access to a wider audience and a larger pool of prospects. That's because the sites to which you post are also trying to increase their traffic. You piggyback on their marketing efforts *at no cost*. To see how this works, go to UsaJohnson.com. There you'll find numerous articles, all of which may be reprinted at no charge. Our only stipulation is that our names and contact information be provided so prospects know where to contact us. In addition to increasing our hits and links, this approach increases our visibility and credibility.

To find outlets for your work, surf the Web. Identify sites specific to network marketing and/or subjects your prospects would be interested in (e.g., home-based businesses, health, family, finances, retirement, etc.). What publishing opportunities, if any, do these sites offer? Do they accept "outside articles," guest columns or e-newsletter items? If so, make contact.

By the way, if other sites offer high-quality material for free, consider posting it at your site. (Get permission first, of course, and give full attribution.) It's a great way to give your site depth and keep it current.

The write stuff

All Web sites must have visual appeal but that's not enough, for while graphics may attract visitors, your text is what keeps them there. Accordingly:

- Write for "scan-ability." Surfers scan rather than read blocks of text. In fact, one study found that only 16 percent of users read pages word-for-word.

- Cut text to the bone. As a rule, use half the number of words you'd use in offline material. Keep sentences and paragraphs short. Aim for one thought per paragraph.

- Use bolded keywords, subheads, bullets and/or numbers to create "breathing room" and move the eye along.

- Use the active voice.

- Speak in terms of benefits.

- Use vocabulary that all visitors will understand.

- **Be creative.** Anything goes when it comes to the Web. It's there to help you reach your goals. So why not reach them in style — *your* style? Create a site that reflects your personality and mission, your expertise and enthusiasm. Have some serious fun with it.

How to top billing

Search engines make life easy for those seeking information, but they don't guarantee results for businesses that register with them. That's because only 16 percent of all sites are listed with search engines. Can you imagine how many more entries we would all have to sift through if all sites were? No wonder search engines are backlogged, some by months. What can you do in the meantime? Advertise. Here are some options:

- **Pay for position.** In supermarkets, manufacturers pay to have their goods placed favorably. Search engines work much the same way, which is why savvy network marketing companies pay to have the No. 1 spot on search result lists. For example, if you were to conduct a search for "network marketing" and "toys," the XYZ Toy Company would be the first of the 800 sites retrieved. The Web's most popular search engines and sites charge big bucks for placement, which is why most network marketers put their resources elsewhere, or seek out less-frequented engines.

- **Click-throughs.** These look and read like classified ads and are found on the pages that report search results. Click on the classified and you are taken directly to the advertiser's site. Fees for this service vary tremendously, from 10 cents to $10 to thousands of dollars. Shop around to get the best deal.

    Are click-throughs effective? It all depends on how you define the term. For example, we know a graphic designer who used click-throughs to increase traffic to her site. An increase in visitors didn't mean an increase in customers, however. Still, she thinks she's gotten her money's worth. "People don't hire a designer without shopping around," she says. "At least I got them into my store, so to speak. These are prospective customers I never would have met. One day some will return, and when they do, they'll hire me and likely tell others about my services. In that sense, then, my ads will have more than paid for themselves."

- **"Pop-ups" and "pop-unders."** The former pop onto your screen in front of the page you're viewing. Pop-unders do the same, but beneath the page. People find pop-unders less annoying, but like pop-ups, their effectiveness is questionable. Responding to the complaints of customers, some of the major search engines are curtailing or banning their use. According to Leslie Walker of *The Washington Post*, Google and iVillage have dropped them outright. (A recent survey by the latter found that more than 90 percent of its users hated them.) America Online has scaled back their numbers dramatically, and EarthLink now provides its customers with software that blocks them altogether. If all

The greatest ad of all

In today's fast-paced world, word-of-mouth is the best type of ad around. So says James L. Morrison, professor of consumer studies at the University of Delaware.

"[W]e are all overwhelmed by the sheer glut of information," he noted in an *Upline* magazine interview. "We don't know what to listen to or when, and it's getting harder and harder to separate the worthwhile from the waste. That's why it's helpful to have others serve as gatekeepers who control the information and then pass it along."

Keith Laggos, author of *Direct Marketing: An Overview*, concurs. He notes that the average person is bombarded by some 3,000 ads daily via TV, newspapers, radio, magazines, billboards *and* e-mails. The latter have become and will continue to be the largest — and most annoying — source of ads ever.

that doesn't give you pause, know that pop-ups and pop-unders can be expensive.

■ **"Rich media" ads.** There's a new generation of ads that may be worth exploring — "rich media" ads, which make use of video or animation. As FSB (*Fortune Small Business* magazine) reported, these ads can appear at the top of a page, walk across it or insert themselves into the middle of an article. Research conducted by Dynamic Logic found these ads were twice as memorable as static banner ads. Whether surfers like them or find them intrusive is yet to be seen.

■ **Banner ads.** Banner ads are the "billboards" posted at the top or sides of a Web page. Prominent as they be, they're less obtrusive than pop-ups because they don't interfere with your ability to navigate. The more popular a site, the higher the banner ad rate.

Banner ads may be worth exploring at sites that are specific to your business (e.g., those targeted to entrepreneurs, stay-at-home moms, downsized professionals, retirees, etc.).

■ **Classifieds.** On the Web, classifieds work much the same way they do offline. Many online newsgroups and bulletin boards post them, oftentimes for free; so do service providers like AOL. Explore your options.

Getting prospects to come to you

Prequalification via the Web. If that's a concept you do not yet know, you will soon. Its premise is sound, and if our experience is any indication, the results are promising.

Prequalification — also known as opt-in marketing or permission marketing — saves time and money because it allows you to home in on your hottest prospects, namely those who have already expressed interest in your type of opportunity. How do you find these individuals? One of two ways.

The first works like a direct mail campaign except that here there's no stationery to print, no envelopes to address and stamp. Your mail goes out immediately and simultaneously to hundreds, thousands ... even millions. Lists of names can be purchased outright from direct mail companies like www.liszt.com, www.postmasterdirect.com, etc. They can also be purchased for set time periods (e.g., one to three months). The longer and/or more specialized the list, the higher your rental or purchase fees.

What's the expected return rate? According to Seth Godin, author of *Permission Marketing: Turning Strangers Into Friends and Friends into Customers* (Simon & Schuster, 1999), 70 percent of recipients will read at least part of their permission-granted e-mail; 35 percent will actually respond. Godin considers this an impressive rate compared to direct snail-mail campaigns, the most successful of which garner a 1 to 5 percent return rate.*

In addition to direct mail outfits, you can work with Web-based companies that generate leads for a monthly fee to distributors. These are not any old leads, however, but ones targeted to your specific business. Here's how the system works: Through direct e-mail lists and other correspondence, prequalification companies draw visitors to their site. There prospects answer a series of questions to assess their commitment to building a successful home-based business that generates serious income. Those who pass the "quiz" with flying colors proceed to the next level of prequalifying questions; those who don't are politely shown to the door.

---

* We culled these figures from an October 1999 article in *Entrepreneur* magazine. Given the exponential growth of the Web, we suspect the return rate has decreased substantially. No wonder. All of us are being bombarded daily with scores of unsolicited offers hawking every kind of business and product imaginable. No wonder, too, that all of us, on average, toss 95–98 percent of the e-mail we receive.

A pox on spam!

Don't you just love going to your mailbox and having to deal with a pile of junk mail? How many of these pieces wind up in the trash as soon as you're back inside your door? Quite a few, we'd guess. Imagine then the number of junk e-mails each of us receives daily and how many we toss without a glance. This junk, in Internet terms, is called spam, and most recipients find it not just annoying but a total turn-off. They also find it offensive. No day seems to pass when they don't get mail from quacks, pornographers ... you name it.

Understandably, Internet providers are developing software to block these mailings and the government is pursuing ways to outlaw them. Let's hope they do it soon, for recent figures show the problem is quickly getting worse. For example, between September 2001 and July 2002, the volume of junk mail jumped from 8 percent to 35 percent, thanks in part to the low cost of spamming software ($200 and up) and mailing lists ($5 for every million names).What's even more distressing are all the get-rich-quick e-mails that attract those hardest hit by economic downturns. Legitimate network marketing companies get caught in the shuffle, making it difficult and at times impossible for prospects to discriminate between the two.

The bottom line then: Can the spam. Any "mass mailings" you conduct should be sent to prequalified prospects only, namely individuals who specifically requested information on home-based business opportunities.

But that's not all. During this process, prospects also indicate the types of business opportunities they are most interested in (e.g., beauty or nutritional products, legal or telephone services, etc.). Based on their responses, they are directed to the appropriate distributors. Distributors then contact these prospects via e-mail. To get a demonstration of how this system works, visit www.MaxOut.com.*

> ## At the very least ...
>
> When prospects respond to an opt-in mailing, get as much contact information from them as possible, at a minimum: name, e-mail address, phone number. This allows you to address them more personally in subsequent contacts. As we all know, people are more responsive when called by their names.

Given the success of these systems, distributors are launching their own prequalification sites. They too purchase prospect lists and send out e-mailings with links to their site. Visitors take a quiz and those who "pass" are contacted. Some distributors take the system one step further. Any leads they get are passed on to their downline on a rotating basis.

As great as prequalification sounds, don't expect thousands, or even hundreds, of prospects to come knocking on your door. And even if they did, there's no guarantee any would become distributors. In that respect, prequalification is like any other recruitment tool. Nonetheless, it is an important one because it separates the wheat from the chaff, so to speak, allowing you to put your energies where they have the greatest potential for return.

Another caveat: Don't expect to hit pay dirt with a single mailing or contact. It generally takes between three and 12 mailings/

---

* Although we are not promoting any specific site or service in this chapter, we are including examples of those that can find, contact and manage prospects — just to illustrate how much help there is out there to build your business.

contacts before a distributor signs up. Accordingly, Kim Klaver suggests that you create a series of e-mails. "Effective e-mail marketing is like dating," she writes in her book *Do You Have a Plan B?* "Getting to know each other takes more than one date, does it not? Who really wants to be thought of as a one-night e-mail stand? No one wants to think they're that easy. And if they are, how good do you think they'll be? How long will they last? Easy come, easy go."

How to use (and not use) e-mail to your advantage

- **Pay attention to your subject line.** This is your grabber. It should be laser-like in its appeal. Ideally, it will showcase your competitive advantages by summarizing the contents of your e-mail. You have fewer words than you think. (Example: Instead of "I am responding to your request," try "Your requested info".)

- **Be brief and direct.** As with Web sites, individuals skim rather than read e-mails. Therefore, make the first couple of sentences in your e-mail winners. (Example: Instead of "Many people want to start a business from their home but don't know how," try "Launching a home-based business is easier than you think.")

- **Don't make sensational or false claims.** They're unethical, illegal and a total turn-off. Further, they give our profession a bad name.

- **Personalize e-mails as much as possible.** Short of using names, sprinkle the word "you" throughout the body of your note. (Example: Instead of "Studies show that 75 percent of all employees want to work from home," try "Want to work from home? You're not alone".)

- **Keep your text to a single screen and use as much white space as possible.** Use subheads and special characters to break up text, and cut your copy down to about half what you'd normally write for a non-Internet audience. (See the sidebar at right for samples of special characters.)

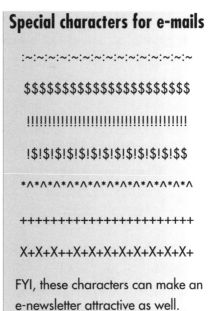

Special characters for e-mails

:~:~:~:~:~:~:~:~:~:~:~:~:~:~

$$$$$$$$$$$$$$$$$$$$$$$$$$

!!

!$!$!$!$!$!$!$!$!$!$!$!$!$$

^^*^*^*^*^*^*^*^*^*^*^*^

++++++++++++++++++++++++

X+X+X++X+X+X+X+X+X+X+X+

FYI, these characters can make an e-newsletter attractive as well.

- **Don't use all caps.** It's the equivalent of online shouting. Use asterisks for emphasis instead. (Before: "SPECIAL DEAL!" After: "**Special Deal!**")

- **Never, ever send an e-mail en masse without using a bcc (blind copy).** Don't violate your prospects' privacy. If you don't know how to create a bcc, consult your program's help section and/or contact your Web host for assistance.

- **Avoid attachments.** Attachments, especially those containing graphics, can take forever to download. If possible, provide links to your site or others where the same material can be viewed. There's another reason to avoid attachments: Prospects wary of viruses won't open them and may well simply trash your e-mail before it's read.

- **Can the spam.** Any "mass mailings" you send should be to prequalified prospects only. No ifs, ands or buts. Anything else you send is spam, and make no mistake, recipients hate it. It's obnoxious, off-putting, and increasingly, a violation of privacy.

- **Create a signature line.** Instead of ending your e-mail with "Sincerely, John Doe," add a tag line to tell others more about who you are, what you do and how to get in touch. Your signature line should be no more than six lines. Use more than that, and prospects may feel you're coming on too strong. Example:

> John Doe, Independent Distributor for XYZ
> Health, wealth and happiness are just a phone call away.
> www.JohnDoe.com
> Questions?@JohnDoe.com
> Phone: (212) XXX-XXXX
> Fax: (212) XXX-XXXX

- **Use autoresponders.** As their name implies, autoresponders respond automatically to a prospect's queries. You pen the response, the system does the rest (with the help of your Web master!).

  Say, for example, that a prospect visits your site and wants to subscribe to your newsletter. He sends an e-mail and — voila! — receives immediate confirmation. Say a prospect wants to learn more about your new product line. No sooner does her e-mail reach you than your information is sent to her. Imagine the time this could save you!

  Autoresponders are also a great way to keep in touch. You can use them to keep prospects abreast of company events, or to let them know the best times to reach you. This is particularly important should you go out of town. In that case, your autoreponse might read:

Thanks for getting in touch. I'm out of the office but will be back on Tuesday and would love to connect. I'll drop you a line then to set up a time to talk. In the meantime, stop by my Web site — www.xyz.com. You'll learn more about my business opportunity and how I can help you launch a successful home-based business. Looking forward to talking with you!

■ **Launch an e-newsletter.**
E-newsletters are a great
way to promote your
business, build
relationships and keep
prospects in the loop.
They're mailed regularly to
opt-in subscribers looking
for timely and relevant
information.

As editor, you decide
how often you'll publish,
be it monthly, weekly or
daily. Generally, the more
frequent your newsletter,
the shorter it should be.
Subscribers don't want to
read a massive tome, at
least not daily. Even the
shortest of dailies can be
too much to digest.

Don't write to hear the
"sound of your own
voice." Your newsletter
must serve your
subscribers. If it doesn't,
it will be trashed faster
than you can say "spam."

Registration services

Here is a list of places to register
e-newsletters and Web sites,
including registration services and
Web promotion:*

www.lycos.comn

www.infoseek.go.com

www.altavista.com

www.hotbot.com

www.excite.com

www.liszt.com

www.topica.com

www.selfpromotion.com

www.site-see.com

www.autosubmit.com/promote.html

cozycabin.com/addsite.html

www.did-it.com

www.2020tech.com/submit.html

Addresses current as of Spring 2003.

To learn more about newsletters, subscribe to a few. When
you're ready to launch, call in your Web master. He or she will set
up your subscription system and provide on-going circulation
reports.

Other ways to use the Web

Create an e-book

E-books don't have to become bestsellers to pay off big time. An example: At UsaJohnson.com, we offer Usa's autobiography, *A Dream Come True* (Advanced Business Corporation, 2000), as a free e-book. It cost next to nothing to post and is available to everyone, everywhere, 24 hours a day. Prospects can download it within seconds, print it out or read it online. By the time they're done, they've learned a whole lot about Usa and network marketing. Those ready to take the next step get in touch. The response to the book has been nothing short of phenomenal. It's one of our best marketing and prequalifying tools.

Once you've got your content nailed, an e-book is easy to create. Web masters and graphic designers can set one up for you. So can any of the e-book companies now on the Web, many of which will also promote your book via the Internet.

Post to bulletin boards

Unlike the bulletin boards you see at work or your local supermarket, online bulletin boards focus on specific subject areas, be they stamp collecting, politics, health, finance or network marketing. Many also limit themselves to geographic areas.

While a good number of bulletin boards are advertiser-supported and thereby free, many others charge annual membership fees. Members use the service to share and receive information in keeping with their interests. Although you can't post direct ads (unless you pay for them and they're labeled as such), you can craft listings that get your point across in more subtle and intriguing ways.

To explore the world of bulletin boards, begin at one of the major search engines. Click on the subjects your prospects would be most interested in (e.g., technology, health and beauty, food, etc.), then post away.

Participate in discussion groups (a.k.a. newsgroups and forums)

Discussion groups work much like bulletin boards in that they focus on specific topics. Here, however, you post messages that other group members can read and respond to. Your message can't hawk a particular company, product or service. However, you can share information indirectly.

For example, say you represent a company that sells health products and you belong to a health-related newsgroup. While you can't write, "Try XYZ and you'll cure arthritis," you can say, "I've tried every arthritis remedy under the sun, but nothing helped until recently, when I found a new product that has truly worked wonders for me. I don't want to plug any company here, but if you want more information, just e-mail me and I'll be happy to share what I know."

Chat online

Chat rooms are just that — on-line, real-time discussions in which individuals exchange text messages. One person makes a comment via keyboard and others respond. The number of chat room participants can range from a handful to several hundred.

Although most chat rooms are free-for-all discussions,* making

---

*Some chat room discussions are moderated, meaning there is someone in charge of maintaining decorum and censoring obscenities and defamatory statements.

them of questionable value as a marketing tool, there are some groups devoted to topics that would be of particular appeal to prospects. Again, and as with bulletin boards and discussion groups, you can't make an outright sales pitch. You can, however, be subtle.

For example, say you're in a chat room devoted to women's fashions and visitors are discussing makeup and allergies. You could raise the importance of finding just the right line of high-quality allergen-free brands. The discussion might then turn to suggestions of specific brands. It's there that you can step in.

You've only just begun

Although we've provided solid information on the wild, wonderful Web, we know it's far from comprehensive. Fortunately or not, the Web is a work in progress. Catching up and keeping up is quite a challenge. But it's one worth meeting.

How to keep abreast? Keep your eyes and ears open. Surf a bit each day to see what's hot or not, what works or doesn't. Read all you can, if only to familiarize yourself with Internet terms. Talk to techno-geeks to learn what's on the horizon and to everyday folks to see what's in current use. Last but not least, take a deep breath! You don't have to do everything at once. Small steps, giant leaps — both will move you forward.

Three ways we've used these strategies

1. We were not among the first wave of network marketers to tap the Internet. Nor were we among the second, third or fourth waves. We came to the Web somewhat reluctantly, and not just because of the learning curve involved. We were slow because we didn't quite understand how the Web could build our organization, if it could at all. Weren't computers too impersonal in a business that relied so heavily on one-on-one contact?

We quickly grew enamored with this new medium, however — all it could do, the numbers of people it could reach. Which is not to say we weren't aware of its limitations, as mentioned at the beginning of this chapter. That's why we continue to work, in great part, in more traditional ways. We recommend that you do the same.

We also recommend that you become Web savvy. Your prospects are, so you'd better keep pace. You need not become a techno-geek, however. Leave the sophisticated stuff to programmers and designers, not to mention your company, whose site will (or should) incorporate the Internet's latest and greatest features. Instead, simply tool around the Web. Only when we got a sense of how it all worked could we brainstorm ways to tap its potential.

To do so, we visited hundreds of network marketing sites to learn all we could from colleagues and competitors. We used a variety of search engines to better understand the differences among them. We subscribed to e-newsletters to study the many ways they were used to convey information, promote business opportunities and products, and create a sense of community among subscribers. We downloaded e-books and PDF files to review their quality and effectiveness. We tuned into video and audio programs to determine if they lived up to the hype. We absorbed.

We can't emphasize enough how important this is. You simply must do the same or you'll put yourself at an enormous disadvantage. You will literally cut yourself off from prospects be they across the street or across the globe.

2. Alas, we can't be in two places at once, especially not when that second place is Thailand, where Usa's downline is growing exponentially. Although she travels overseas several times a year, sometimes for weeks at a time, she does the bulk of her work from our home in Maryland, the majority of it via telephone.

It can make for a grueling schedule, as there is a 12-hour time difference between the two countries. Partly it's the nature of the Thai culture, where one-on-one contact is perhaps even more critical than it is in the United States. E-mail just wouldn't cut it in terms of prospecting or staying in touch with distributors (who, in essence, are among our greatest prospecting tools).

We mention this to illustrate how the Web will *not* help us grow our business in Thailand, at least not by itself. We suspect this will change, but not in the next few months or perhaps years. As here, it takes time for people to flatten their learning curve and/or gain access to computers.

And so we use the phone, a somewhat low-tech medium but a more effective one for our purposes. All of which is to say that you don't need a whole lot of bells and whistles to get down to business. Think about that the next time you feel pressured to jump aboard the Web train as it barrels past.

3. One of the most exciting things about the Web is how it has opened the world to us. We're not just talking prospects here, but information. From our home computer we can tap into literally tens of thousands of resources that can help us build our business. For example, when we want to update the figures found on Pages 53–54, we can do so in moments by visiting the American Marketing Association (www.marketingpower.com), Direct Marketing Association (www.the-dma.org) or the Direct Sellers Association (www.dsa.org). When we want to locate books on cold-calling techniques, we can skim titles at Amazon.com. When we want to learn more about business or population trends, we can zip over to *Entrepreneur* magazine (www.entrepreneur.com) or the U.S. Census Bureau (www.census.gov), respectively .

If you have not yet tapped this gold mine, do so ASAP. You will be amazed and empowered by what you find.

Part 4

Success revealed

Chapter 8

Our No. 1 Prospecting Tool

You have now come to what we believe is the most important chapter in this book. Here we reveal the ultimate secret to our prospecting success — and yours. It can be summed up in a single word: *belief*. After 30 combined years in the business, we credit all of our achievements to that one word.

Belief, however, is not something you learn by rote or plan. It rises slowly within, like the sun at dawn, brushing away the shadows and revealing a world full of possibilities.

Each day, when we rise, we find greater possibilities still. For this we have to thank our many "teachers" — the take-charge, positive-thinking individuals whose wise words and courageous acts allowed us to see beyond our horizons. Through their tapes, books and our personal associations, we've come to understand that everything's possible if you believe it is. How simple a concept! How challenging as well. To act on your belief is akin to working without a net; what if you fall? Ah, but what if you don't? What if, instead, you form wings and soar to the greatest of heights?

That is what we wish for you, and that is why

Quotes of note

Here and on the pages that follow are some of our favorite quotations. Read and use them as we do — as nuggets of wisdom that will remind you of life's riches, within and without.

■

Faith is to believe what we do not see; and the reward of this faith is to see what we believe.
—*St. Augustine*

■

The man who says "It can't be done" is interrupted by the man who is doing it.
—*Unknown*

we're sharing the key concepts that shaped our belief system.

Wealth is a state of mind

Even as children, we pondered how others had achieved great wealth. Were they born into it? Did they possess a special gene or God-given talent? Were they just lucky? With time, we learned the answers.

Yes, some individuals are born into wealth; a greater number, however, come from modest or less-than-modest means. Their wealth is self-made, born of vision and hard work.

No, there is no one gene that sets the wealthy apart from the not-so-wealthy. Biologically, we are all alike. No one is born with a lock on talent. God gave each of us many talents, and it is our duty to use them.

Yes and no regarding luck. Sometimes events conspire in positive ways. To a greater degree, however, we make our own luck. We create wealth through our mind-set. Think rich and you will draw riches to you.

While some of these riches can be measured in dollars and cents, others are measured by quality of life. Doing what you love, being with those you love, having the time and space to enjoy the world around you — these are gifts money can't buy. Nonetheless, with the right attitude, you can have them all, and then some. Believing makes it so.

Ask and you shall receive

Life, we believe, is one long birthday party. You get new gifts each day, and if you're smart you open them. That's one of the reasons why we love the tale recounted in both *The Prayer of Jabez* and *The Science of Getting Rich.** To paraphrase:

> *A man dies and goes to heaven, where he is greeted by St. Peter, who shows him around. During this tour, the man notices a building that looks like a warehouse. St. Peter takes him inside and there, in row after row, are boxes that each bear an individual's name. Curious as to what is in the box with his name,*

Don't be afraid of opposition. Remember, a kite rises against, not with, the wind.
—*Hamilton Mabie*

■

Don't fall victim to what I call the ready-aim-aim-aim syndrome. You must be willing to fire.
—*T. Boone Pickens*

■

You've got to have a dream if you're going to make a dream come true.
—*Denis Waitley*

---

* *The Prayer of Jabez: Breaking Through to the Blessed Life* by Bruce Wilkinson (Multnomah Publishers, Inc., 2000); *The Science of Getting Rich* by Wallace D. Wattles and Dr. Judith Powell (Top of the Mountain Pub., 2002).

A map of the world that does not include Utopia is not even worth glancing at.
—Oscar Wilde

■

Take risks. Safeway is a grocery store.
—Joey Reiman

■

We don't see things as they are. We see them as we are.
—Talmud

the man lifts its cover to find all the blessings God had reserved for him. "Why were they not mine when I was alive?" he asks, to which St. Peter sadly replies, "You never asked for them."

The moral of this story is clear: Your life, here and now, is full of riches and always will be. Accept and use them.

Abundance abounds

There isn't enough to go around.

My gain is another person's loss.

It is wrong to want more.

These statements are examples of what Shakti Gawain calls scarcity programming. As she notes in her classic book, *Creative Visualization,** the statements assume the universe is finite, that we're each given a slice of the pie, and the only way we can have more is to take it from others.

False, false, false. Life is not a pie; it is a feast available to all. You step up to the table by choice, and it is the correct one. It is your way of acknowledging the many

---

* *Creative Visualization: Use the Power of Your Imagination to Create What You Want in Your Life* (New World Library, 2002).

gifts life offers and accepting them with grace. If you don't, you will limit yourself — and others.

That's because life is abundant and we are all naturally prosperous. As Gawain says, those who don't understand this have "bought into the popular belief in the inevitability of poverty and lack, and do not realize yet that the ultimate power of creating rests in the hands (or rather hearts) of each of us." Therefore, having what you want, enjoying the feast so to speak, contributes to the general state of human happiness. As a result, you help others create more happiness for themselves.

Isn't it time you enjoyed the infinite banquet life offers?

Create a better world

If at first you don't succeed, you're running about average. That's one of our favorite quotes, and we share it often with those new to network marketing. As we impress upon them, there's no such thing as overnight success, just a whole lot of daytime victories.

To be victorious you must accept the challenges ahead. There will be times when you will question yourself. It would be abnormal if you didn't. But don't succumb to the response of so many,

There are two kind of people in the world — those who walk into a room and say "There you are," and those who say "Here I am!"
—Abigail Van Buren

First you jump off the cliff, then you build your wings on the way down.
—Ray Bradbury

Once you make a decision, the universe conspires to make it happen.
—Ralph Waldo Emerson

Courage is doing what
you're afraid to do.
There can be no
courage unless you're
scared.
—*Eddie Rickenbacker*

▪

Our mental attitude is
the X factor that
determines our fate.
—*Dale Carnegie*

▪

If you aren't going all
the way, why go at all?
—*Joe Namath*

▪

which is to walk away. Failure is not due
to a lack of success, but a lack of effort.
That's why it's so important that you
hang in there one moment longer. That
one moment can change your life.

Read biographies of the world's
greatest political and business leaders,
scientists and artists, and you'll quickly
understand the importance of stick-to-it-
ive-ness. Where would our world be had
they given in to doubt? Where would we
be if you too gave in? Your success makes
possible the success of others. That's the
beauty of the network marketing model.
By staying the course, you help create a
better world.

Visualize your future

Visualization, alone or coupled with
affirmations, is a potent and enjoyable
tool for realizing your dreams. As the
term suggests, you visualize a positive
outcome (in your case, wealth), making
its "picture" so compelling that you
experience it with all your senses. Put
another way, visualization gives you a
peek into the future you will create, a
future you will draw to you.

Whatever you want in life begins first
with a thought. You think: I want to
switch careers. I want to earn in the six-
figures. I want to retire in style. These

thoughts create the reality. If you didn't think them, let alone acknowledge them, you couldn't have them.

Visualization is more than daydreaming, however. It takes a bit of work. You must not only identify what you want, but do so in detail. For example, say you work in sales for a mid-size company and you're burning out fast. You're working 10-hour days, on the road nearly two weeks out of every month and still struggling to support your family. That new home you wanted will have to be put off yet another year, as will saving for your retirement. And forget the vacation you've promised your kids. No way will you have the time or money.

How would you visualize a better life? By creating a new reality that all five senses experience in the present. The new version might go as follows:

> I wake in the morning to watch the sun rise from the deck of my beachfront home. The waves dash onto the beach as the sandpipers race across the sand. The air is crisp and salty, the sky a perfect shade of blue. I hear my spouse stir and I go inside to make us coffee. We sit at the table, having a relaxed conversation and planning the day ahead.

Intention + Attention = Miracles
—*Unknown*

■

The only place where success comes before work is in the dictionary.
—*Vidal Sassoon*

■

Destiny is not a matter of chance, it is a matter of choice. It is not a thing to be waited for, it is a thing to be achieved.
—*Jeremy Kitson*

In each of us are places where we have never gone. Only by pressing the limits do you ever find them.
—*Dr. Joyce Brothers*

■

You can have anything you want if you want it desperately enough. You must want it with an exuberance that erupts through the skin and joins the energy that created the world.
—*Sheila Graham*

I head into my office overlooking the dunes. It's the start of an unpressured work day. I begin with phone calls to key members of my downline. I love to hear their voices, to know they are part of my life. Together, we share ideas and goals.

With calls done, I play my favorite CDs and finish some paperwork. I break midday, and after lunch go for my daily walk along the ocean. I breathe deeply, contentedly, my heart full of joy and gratitude.

Doesn't sound bad, eh? And no, it's not a fantasy. You can have this kind of life — and any other you visualize. But first, you have to really see it, feel it, know it.

Take a few moments to visualize what you most want. Close your eyes and let your heart soar. See it all in as much detail as possible. Don't judge or scale back your dreams. Follow where they lead.

Once these images are clear, embed them in your mind. Think of them as a snapshot you can gaze upon regularly during relaxed moments of your day. As you do, remember that thought always precedes manifestation.

Affirm your dreams

Affirmations are potent tools to develop the right mind-set. Through them you affirm, verbally or in writing — *and in the present tense* — that which you want. This latter point is critical, for affirmations must be phrased not as wishes but as statements of fact.

Often you'll have to go beyond the facts at hand. For example, say you want to be wealthy. OK, but what if your definition of wealth goes beyond dollars and cents? Obviously, you can't buy happiness. Perhaps then it isn't just wealth you want, but an enjoyment of everyday life and the people within it. You want new experiences, to learn all you can about all you can. You want to help others, to feel that in the end you mattered. To you, *that* is real wealth. Can you see then how saying "I am rich" doesn't express your true desires?

Instead, you might want to substitute the word prosperity. But even saying "I am prosperous" doesn't quite cut it. There's no real emotion to it; prosperity, here, is just an object, not unlike a chair. But what if you began to play with your words:

I enjoy prosperity ... My life is prosperous ... I have all I want and give all I have ... I am living a golden life.

> Know your limits, not so that you can honor them, but so that you can smash them to pieces and reach for magnificence.
> —*Cherie Carter-Scott*

■

> [Y]ou have to pay close attention to what you love, and never listen to anyone who tells you to be practical too early in the game.
> —*Barbara Sher*

Okay, Universe. Take
over, please. Take me
where you wish. I'll enjoy
the ride.
—*Susan Jeffers*

■

I've always tried to go a
step past wherever
people expected me to
end up.
—*Beverly Sills*

You get the idea. So write and rewrite your affirmation. Try out several versions to discover which one most accurately reflects your dreams.

Play the Part

We've all heard the expression, "fake it 'til you make it." We find the concept helpful, but only in part. See, we believe you don't have to fake anything. You, like your goals, are authentic. If prosperity is what you want, then simply play the part of a prosperous person.

For example:

If you dream of having a great wardrobe, wear the nicest clothes you have no matter where you go (to work, a concert, the grocery store).

If you dream of eating in fine restaurants, forgo fast foods and save your money for a great meal in an upscale restaurant.

If you dream of having the ideal home, make your present home more attractive by buying a few pieces of attractive furniture or hanging lovely paintings on the walls.

If you dream of monthlong vacations in the south of France, enjoy fun and relaxed weekends in Quebec, or take classes in French cooking, literature or art.

Everything you want has a feel, a quality to it, and you don't have to wait until later to experience it. In fact, when you allow yourself to experience it in the here and now, it becomes a natural part of your life. Prosperity too becomes more natural. You expect to have more of it, and so you will.

Take responsibility

Life's winners know that excuses are a poor investment of time and energy. That's why they toss them faster than junk mail. And so should you. Excuses repel the very wealth you want to attract. How do you purge them? By taking responsibility for your actions … or lack thereof.

Don't point a finger of blame (or should we say fingers of blame?) at your circumstances. To a great extent, circumstances are created, not imposed. Which is not to say you're responsible for your awful childhood or being downsized from your job. Bad things do happen to good people. Still, they don't have to keep happening. At some point you must break with the past, even with the present, if you are to create a promising future.

We suspect you already have, if only in part. You wouldn't have been drawn to

> Thousands of people have talent. I might as well congratulate you for having eyes in your head. The one and only thing that counts is: Do you have staying power?
> —*Noel Coward*

> ∎

> You are your choices.
> —*Jean Paul Sartre*

Tell me to what you pay attention, and I will tell you who you are.
—*Jose Ortega y Gasset*

■

You can't learn anything from experiences you're not having.
—*Louis L'Amour*

■

An obstacle is something you see when you take your eyes off the goal.
—*Sam Horn*

network marketing if you didn't think it could change your life for the better. That thought, as all thoughts, was based on belief. "I can do this," you told yourself. And we say, "Yes, you can, and more."

Make deposits

Imagine you have a wallet filled with 100 one-dollar bills. On the way to work you gassed up the car ($18), picked up a paper and a double espresso ($5), and paid your toll ($4) and daily parking fee ($7). Before 9 a.m. you would already have spent $34, leaving you $66.

Now imagine you also paid $10 for every negative thought you had between waking and getting to your desk:

"That darn alarm clock. I hate waking up early." ($10)

"Oh, great. No clean towels again." ($10)

"I look like crap." ($10)

"I bet I'll get stuck in traffic." ($10)

"That idiot cut me off." ($10)

"Seven bucks for parking. What a rip-off." ($10)

"This elevator takes forever." ($10)

"I bet Bob's going to rope me into that stupid project of his." ($10)

"There's Mary. I'd like to ask her out, but she's only going to say no." ($10)

Hmmm … that's $90. You're running a deficit and it's just after 9 a.m. Can you imagine what you'd owe by the end of the day? Several thousand, we'd guess, and that's being conservative.

Moral: Avoid negative thoughts. At a time when you want to soar, they'll keep you tied to the ground. They'll make you believe the world is conspiring against you and that those within it merely serve to impede and annoy.

Abide by the law of gratitude

We first learned of this law when reading *The Science of Getting Rich.* According to Wattles' law, strong and constant gratitude attracts what you want in life. It is what connects you to the Universal Spirit. "It is like sending a thank-you note to a friend for their thoughtful gift, for which they, in turn, will acknowledge you with a return letter or a telephone call." In other words, the universe responds with gifts of its own.

Gratitude is also important because it gives birth to faith. "The grateful mind continually expects good things, and expectations becomes faith," Wattles

The difference between a successful person and others is not a lack of strength, nor a lack of knowledge, but rather a lack of will.
—*Vince Lombardi*

■

Be like a postage stamp. Stick to it until you get there.
—*Harvey Mackay*

■

Everything comes to him who hustles while he waits.
—*Thomas A. Edison*

Optimists are right. So
are pessimists. It's up
to you to choose which
you will be.
—Harvey Mackay

■

A diamond is a lump of
clay that stuck with it.
—Anonymous

wrote. "One who has no feeling of
gratitude cannot long retain a living faith
— and without faith you cannot get rich
by the creative method." Why then cut
yourself off from the world's riches?

That's why we suggest you buy a
special notebook in which you list all of
the good things in your life. Make your
entries each night so you will awake
with a positive mind-set. Do this for
several days and you will understand
just how many things you have to be
grateful for.

Keep your word

People of integrity keep their word to
others; they also keep their word to
themselves. Put another way, they follow
through on their dreams.

Dreams are promises; they are meant
to be realized, not broken. They are
meant to be acted upon.

But take heed. Action isn't enough.
Say, for example, that you want to be
happy. Wealth might help you achieve
that state, but it can't guarantee it.
Neither can losing weight, switching
careers or getting married. True
happiness can only be achieved through
belief. Know you will be happy, truly
open yourself to it, and it shall be yours.
It is willingness, without a doubt, that

will make miracles happen in your life.

When you are ready and willing, you will be able. That's because you will become a magnet, attracting the very things you've dreamed of. Once you touch them, your dreams become more fully charged and the things you want come to you more and more quickly.

Set a goal, then expand it

When you were a child and going through yet another growth spurt, your parents likely bought you new clothes that were a tad big. They knew you'd grow into them in no time. And so it is with goals. Think big, not small. Why limit your success?

This can be a tricky business because it requires that you not only believe your goals are possible, but also that there are ways to achieve them. It's easier to believe the former; proof abounds. All you have to do is look at your upline or read the many articles and books written by today's top earners. It's the latter that is the real challenge. Certainly it was for us, for it doesn't matter if you know where you want to go if you can't figure out how to get there. *There* can seem light-years away; but trust us, it's not.

> If you can't find a way, make one.
> —*Beth Mende Conny*
>
> ∎
>
> When you take your eyes off yourself and put them on others, your business will grow.
> —*Unknown*
>
> ∎

Anyone who does not believe in miracles is not a realist.
—*David Ben-Gurion*

■

Every strike brings me closer to the next home run.
—*Babe Ruth*

See, most network marketers want to get from:

Here → *There*

That's quite a big leap, especially if you're not used to jumping. But what if you didn't have to make one huge leap? What if instead of getting from *Here* to *There*, you put your energies into getting from A to Z? And what if doing so required merely that you first get from A to B, then B to C, C to D, and so on? A lot less scary, eh?

A → *B* → *C* → *D* ...

Another reason why we like this approach is that it puts things in a new perspective. You better understand the importance of progression and how each step, no matter how small, moves you closer to your ultimate goal. Accomplishment is the greatest confidence-builder around.

Choose good company

Life's short, and there's so much you want to do. That's why you need to avoid those who sap your energy. That may sound heartless, but there's only so much of you to go around. Family, friends, colleagues — all deserve their share. But so do you, so why squander it on individuals who undermine your dreams? These naysayers come in all shapes and sizes. Instead of support, they offer endless reasons why you'll fail. Before you know it, you're wound up and scared, and fast losing sight of your goals.

Unfortunately, you can't purge all of these people from your life — there are far too many of them. Fortunately, you can minimize their influence by drawing positive thinkers into your life. These individuals are dreamers and doers. They want what you want, a rich, full life — and they're willing to go after it. Sure, it will take hard work and sacrifice, but that's a small price to pay. From this standpoint, the naysayers pay a much larger price by settling for so little.

Seek out these positive thinkers. Some may well be in your immediate circle. Others may be down the block, one seat over on a bus or at your next prospecting meeting. Because you'll never know for sure, keep your eyes, ears and mind open. You'll recognize them in a flash. They have a way of walking, talking and smiling that sets them apart. You'll be kindred souls.

Another way to add positive thinkers to your life is to become an avid reader. Bookstore and library shelves are filled

> You get more out of life by trying something and failing than you do by trying nothing and succeeding.
> —*Unknown*

■

> Persistence is what makes the impossible possible, the possible likely, and the likely definite.
> —*Robert Half*

> Make your life a mission
> — not an intermission.
> —*Arnold H. Glasgow*

> ■

> Work is a four-letter word.
> It's up to us to decide
> whether that four-letter
> word read "drag" or
> "love."
> —*Al Sacharov*

> ■

> Ever tried? Ever failed?
> No matter. Try again.
> Fail again. Fail better.
> —*Samuel Beckett*

with excellent titles on self-development, visualization, goal setting and the like. Their authors make great company and offer invaluable words of wisdom. Spend a bit of time with them each day, and you'll find yourself on the fast track to success.

Give all you've got and you'll get all you want

In our minds, the second idea is the more important, even pressing, for as the saying goes, success breeds success. Prospects know whether someone walks the talk or merely crawls. They want to go with winners. Only when you present yourself as such will you truly get their attention. Prospects perceive you as successful. Believe in yourself, and others will believe in you. Put another way, *you* are your best prospecting tool. You can mirror what others want to become.

Put all you've learned to immediate use!

- Each week, reread a specific chapter or section and choose one to three strategies to implement.

- Choose a colleague or your sponsor to help you set —and stick to — your prospecting goals.

- Use this book to create a prospecting training program for your downline.

- Order personalized copies of this book as a marketing tool for recruiting new distributors and customers. Details on the next page!

Absolutely EVERYTHING You Need to Know About Prospecting

Here are two great ways to recruit new distributors, build a loyal customer base and turn your downline into an army of master prospectors!

#1
Order bulk discounted copies of *Absolutely* Everything *You Need to Know About Prospecting.*

#2
Order customized copies that include any or all of the following special features:

- Your name on the cover indicating the book is a personalized gift.

- A biographical chapter to introduce prospects to both you and your organization.

- Additional pages profiling your company, its products and the special business opportunities it offers.

For more information on these special options, contact:

Biz Builders Consulting, LLC
P.O. Box 1936
Frederick, MD 21702
301/694-9921
orders@bizbuildersconsulting.com